The DNA of the Resilient Organization

How One Collective Heartbeat Creates Continuous Competitive Advantage

Sandra A. Suran

STARGAZER
Publishing Company
PO Box 77002
Corona, CA 92877-0100

"Educate, Enlighten, Entertain"

The DNA of the Resilient Organization

Published by Stargazer Publishing Company
PO Box 77002
Corona, CA 92877-0100
(800) 606-7895
(951) 898-4619
FAX (951) 898-4633
Corporate e-mail: stargazer@stargazerpub.com
Order e-mail: orders@stargazerpub.com
website: http://www.stargazerpub.com

Cover design: www.calypso.concepts.com

ISBN: 9781933277219 (Hardcover)
        9781933277196 (trade paper)
        9781933277226 (Kindle)
        9781933277202 (e-Pub)

Contact the author:
www.resiliencedna.com
ssuran@thesurangroup.com
www.thesurangroup.com
Blog: www.surangroup.com

Library of Congress Cataloging-in-Publication Data

Suran, Sandra A., 1944-
   The DNA of the resilient organization : how one collective heartbeat creates continuous competitive advantage / Sandra A. Suran.
      pages cm
   Includes bibliographical references.
   ISBN 978-1-933277-21-9 (hardcover) -- ISBN 978-1-933277-19-6 (trade paper) -- ISBN 978-1-933277-22-6 (kindle) -- ISBN 978-1-933277-20-2 (e-pub)
   1. Organizational change. 2. Organizational effectiveness. 3. Strategic planning. I. Title.
   HD58.8.S87 2014
   658.4'06--dc23
                      2013049701

A.M.D.G.

The DNA of the Resilient Organization

Acknowledgements

This book would never have happened without the pushing, coaching, and publishing skills of three key people. Publishers have asked and friends have suggested that I write a book on various topics over the decades, but I never had the the impetus to do it. Three very special people made it happen: one to start the engine, one to get it loaded and moving on the right track, and one to guide it across the tough terrain of publishing and bring it to its final destination.

Dr. Beatrice Aebi-Magee, my good friend, advisor on several particularly challenging projects, and one of the most talented and intuitive executive coaches in the world, assured that this book would get started. She pushed me, as others had, to document my unique approach to organizational change. I said, "I don't know what to write. I don't know what I do differently. I just do what I think is needed to help each organization, individually." Her response was, "I will interview you!" We went to our Club and sat by the fireplace. She brought her laptop, asked questions, and typed my answers. The next day, she sent four single-spaced pages and wrote, "Here is the start of your book!"

It took over two years and the Great Recession for me to develop my concepts into chapters and start thinking about how to publish it. That's when I re-connected with Bob Phillips, talented HR consultant on many of my early projects and recent co-author of *Absolute Honesty*. Like Dr. Aebi-Magee, he suggested that I write a book. When I told him I *was* writing one, he told me about his book agent, the incomparable Michael Snell. Michael introduced me to the world of national publishers and led me through two years of book development, proposal writing and editing, coaching, and encouragement. After he understood what I was trying to say, it was he who suggested the new title, *The DNA of the Resilient Organization,* and wrote the book summary. He took me to the brink of signing a contract and was hugely responsible for my increased sophistication and awareness of what I needed to do to create a successful book.

Carol J. Amato, an author, editor, and college friend, believed in the book and encouraged me to finish it. She connected me with her publisher and guided me through the complex and laborious process of copy-editing, and coached me on page layout, cover design, and distribution. I could not have completed it without her expert guidance!

Peter Senge, without his knowing, has been my guide and coach since he first published *The Fifth Discipline* in the same year I started The Suran Group. Since then, I have read many business books but no other has impacted my work as much as he did. I cannot estimate how many hundreds of times I used his name and quoted him over the last 20-plus years. His work enabled me to take my process-thinking, organizational and technical systems skills, and consciously connect them with my fascination with people — increased awareness of, learning about, and motivating them. I owe Peter Senge a lot and this book gives me an opportunity to thank him publicly.

John Soisson, great writer and founding editor of *Portland,* the award-winning University of Portland magazine, and Peter Van Handel, my talented poet/writer/CPA-brother, voluntarily provided editing help and encouragement in the early stages of the book proposal. Libby Koponen, the professional editor who worked with me on the book proposal, taught me the value of "less is better," refreshed my high-school and college editing skills, helped clarify cumbersome phrases and taught me how to do it myself, and provided counsel about the publishing game during the proposal process.

Brian Doyle, current editor of *Portland,* granted permission to use his wonderful prose about the University of Portland women Pilots soccer team. His words are excerpted throughout the book.

My scores of clients, named and unnamed, opened their organizations to me and provided the challenging projects that enabled me to grow and to learn from them and their people. Obviously, the leaders' desires to improve and to change their companies provided the raw materials for this book product. Without them, there would be no book.

My wonderful assistant, Alisa Hammond (and earlier, Dianne Knight), provided constant support and designed the creative graphics. Alisa also did research, formatting on references, and myriad other tasks. I would not have been able to finish this book without their skills and behind-the-scenes support.

Many other people helped, in so many ways, to make this book happen. My heartfelt thanks to all of you — my wonderful family and friends.

Preface

In the early 90s, I started another company, The Suran Group, focused solely on management consulting. At that same time, I read two books that significantly expanded my thinking about what organizations need to do to successfully grow and improve: Peter Senge's *The Fifth Discipline*[1] and James Belasco's *Teaching the Elephant to Dance*[2].

The philosophies were stunning revelations that changed my approach to helping organizations with strategic planning, organization restructuring, and process and systems improvement. I already had begun to realize that as skilled as I thought I was in the technical and leadership areas required to help effect change, I was missing a major component. I learned, from a series of tough experiences, that nothing happens successfully, and certain not sustainably, if the organization's "rank and file" people don't want it to happen.

My questions were "How do I help individuals and groups to want to change?" and "What keeps them from enthusiastically supporting change?" Those two books gave me the tools to practice the "soft" side of project management, organization development, and process improvement and to incorporate behavioral concepts into the technical consulting steps I had developed earlier within my accounting/consulting firm.

I learned more through experience in applying Senge's and Belasco's concepts and while working with my employees, alliance partners, and subcontractors in information/technology systems, human resources, marketing, law, industrial psychology, and process improvement. Another influential, very practical book that I read was *Diagnostic Interviewing for Consultants and Auditors*.[3] This helped me to further expand my listening skills, originally honed while performing complex audits in my CPA firm.

The DNA of the Resilient Organization analyzes my experiences over the past two decades with scores of for-profit, not-for-profit, and governmental organizations of different sizes and in a wide variety of industries. The example scenarios describe real company situations and personalities, although many stories are composites. Names and descriptions of most are camouflaged to respect the privacy of the individuals and entities involved.

The process I use to help organizations plan and implement changes is very individualized. *The DNA of the Resilient Organization* describes the essential components and attributes needed to build healthy, growth-focused, and sustainable organizations — *resilient organizations*. Chapter 7 — *Infrastructure* and *Chapter 8 — People Focus* standardize the basic approach I use to inculcate these attributes in the organization's culture while leading entities through successful changes.

The Chapter Road Map — the Pyramid
There is no quick, easy formula for accomplishing organizational resilience, but utilizing the process detailed in this book with every change effort will increasingly embed resilience attributes within the entity's culture and also develop its proficiency in making changes. A Pyramid map, as shown on the next page, is provided on the first page of every chapter to guide you in learning and linking the process and the attributes needed for resilience. Each chapter's topic is highlighted on the pyramid.

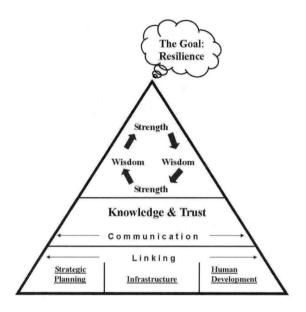

Key Definitions

Stakeholders vs. Employees - *The DNA of the Resilient Organization* applies to all organizations. The road to resilience and manner of dealing with stakeholders is the same for large or small for-profit, not-for-profit, and governmental entities.

I use **"stakeholders"** to mean those who work with and are interested in an entity's success: major suppliers and customers, Board members, and employees. **"Employees"** means stakeholders who are directly involved in operations: management and staff and also volunteers who participate in accomplishing the mission of not-for-profits.

Businesses often use other words interchangeably without differentiating their meanings. The following definitions reflect my use of these words.

Environment vs. Culture - Environment refers to "the conditions that surround someone or something and affect the growth, health, progress, etc. of someone or something" (Merriam Webster Dictionary, 2013). In contrast, **Culture** is "a way of think-ing, behaving, or working that exists in a place or organization" (Merriam Webster Dictionary, 2013).

Information vs. Data – Although these words are often used as synonyms, they differ hugely in impact and usefulness. **Information** is a summary of useful facts about someone or something gained from investigation, study, instruction, or analysis. I define **data** as raw pieces and bits — statistics collected together for reference or analysis (e.g., expenditures, sales, and inventory reports).

Knowledge vs. Wisdom – **Knowledge** includes "facts, information, and skills acquired . . . through experience or education; the theoretical or practical understanding of a subject" (Oxford Dictionaries, 2013). The following definition of **Wisdom** is most consistent with my personal view of it. Wisdom ". . . is a habit or disposition to perform the action with the highest degree of adequacy under any given circumstance. This involves an understanding of people, things, events, and situations, and the willingness and the ability to apply perceptions, judgments, and actions [to determine] the right course of actions. It often requires control of one's emotional reactions...so that universal principles, values, reason, and knowledge prevail to determine one's actions. In short, wisdom is a disposition to find the truth coupled with an optimum judgment as to right actions" (Wikipedia, 2013).

Processes vs. Systems – Processes are "A series of actions or steps taken in order to achieve a parti-cular end (Oxford Dictionaries, 2013). **Systems** are "A set of things working together as parts of a mechanism or an interconnecting network; a com-plex whole (Oxford Dictionaries, 2013).

Contents

Part 3 – Unity

INTRODUCTION

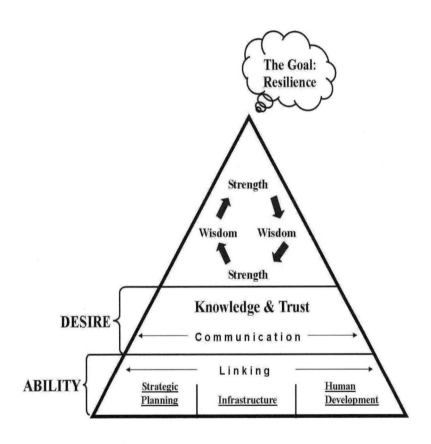

Introduction: Wonder Glue
Enabling Organizations to
Thrive in Times of Challenge

The last time the University of Oregon Ducks football team remained undefeated after eight games was in 1933. They have *never* been #1 in the country. They accomplished both for the first time in 2010.

How did they do it? Look at the big October, 2010, game that put them undisputedly in the #1 spot for the first time ever: the game against their major rival and football powerhouse, University of Southern California's Trojans. The Ducks won 53-32. But it is the *way* they won that explains their greatness — against the unbelievers and especially against the complex computer poll that withheld that ranking even when human polls recognized their special talent.

The Ducks were down going into the second quarter, left the field down by two touchdowns at the end of the half, came back in the third quarter to lead, then went down again in the third quarter — again by two touchdowns. Lesser teams might have been demoralized to be so far behind so late in the game, especially with their record against USC.

In the last 38 years of their contests, the Ducks won only eight times. And now they were playing in the fabled L.A. Coliseum filled with 86,000 rabid, deafeningly mind-numbing Trojan fans. The Ducks had won here only once before in history.

But the Ducks were not demoralized. Each time they fell behind, they calmly, determinedly came back with new moves, different plays. To quote the *Oregonian,* "Just when it looked to all the world like the Ducks were in trouble, they answered with two long, well-designed drives that sucked the air out of the Coliseum and took the momentum away from USC." The Ducks simply wore down the Trojans.

According to Oregon's offensive coordinator, Mark Helfrich, "We came off the sidelines and said, 'This happened, that happened. Fix it. Let's go.' It was just a matter-of-fact approach."[1] The Ducks learned "Resilience."

How did they do it? Chip Kelly, who was only in his second year as Head Coach, did away with the traditional football "huddle" and instead focused on a smart quarterback who knew how to lead, was fearless and would do anything to win. At the same time, Chip focused on *unifying* the team. He also demanded heavy endurance training, personal discipline and extensive practice to think around obstacles as a unit — As One — to follow the quarterback or to follow whoever was leading at the moment because Chip's process built all players to lead when needed. As a result, the Team totally trusted each other — their common training and knowledge, their ability to act with a collective heartbeat, their leaders. Against odds, they could pick themselves up in any situation and confidently, calmly move forward.

The story of NIKE is similar. NIKE was on the verge of bankruptcy three times as they built the company. Every time, they came up with something new and very risky, not safe or already tried by others. And, each time, it worked and they went on to new heights and gained greater stature as a company and greater market share.

Resilience Makes the Difference

How did NIKE do it? It took Resilience – strength in adversity; the ability to bounce back to full strength in difficult situations. Where and how did Nike build that organizational Resilience? They trusted each other and their leaders: Phil Knight, Bill Bowerman and others Phil and Bill later brought into the company. Phil and Bill had absolute trust in one another. Bill knew about building a strong team from his job as a track coach at the University of Oregon; Phil knew about business success and good management from his background as a CPA at Price Waterhouse. From their backgrounds in competitive sports, Bill and Phil knew about performing despite fear. They had the discipline to do whatever it takes for the team to win. Phil sold shoes from the trunk of his car.[2] So the NIKE team, brought together by Phil, knew what to do in adversity and totally trusted their leaders.

The team kept learning and changing, without fear and despite significant roadblocks and potentially destructive challenges. For example, when the terrible working conditions for the employees of NIKE's subcontractors in developing countries were exposed, it appeared that the world would turn against NIKE and their products. The subcontractor problem could have destroyed NIKE. But instead of fighting to defend themselves and shooting arrows at others as many companies in similar situations do, NIKE embraced the problem. They changed their approach to subcontractors. They improved their company because of a great challenge that might have buried their competitors.

This common theme — what enables Resilience and sustainable growth — is also demonstrated in a highly complex socio-ecological system in nature: ant colonies. Ants are adaptable and resilient. Ants are ecologically dominant in all but the coldest areas on the planet. There are over 10,000 types of ants that have adapted internally to cope with all but the most difficult environments on earth. They exist solely for the purpose of foraging or for predation (depending on the availability of food). Ants have one purpose in life: to work cooperatively to help the colony thrive and grow.[3]

Ants are expert at using internal and external cues to adapt their collective lives to the environment. So, what is most interesting and useful to us humans is their ability to adapt and change their roles, lives and social structures as needed to meet challenges and needs.[4,5] They also have a culture of *resilience* that is based on the welfare of the collective entity.

Sounds familiar, right? Both NIKE and the Oregon Ducks used those attributes to win — again and again — despite difficult challenges and odds.

It takes much more than a great leader; it takes more than a great plan to enable consistent success in achieving goals and remaining strong, despite the constant challenges that beset all organizations, because leaders leave and plans change. It takes total, deep understanding by the entire organization of the appropriate moves and assigned tasks and how they link: group *wisdom.* And it takes *strength* (built from trust in the leaders and in each other) and trust that everyone has the skills and will do what is needed when it is needed.

Control and supervision don't assure good performance. Group wisdom and strength relentlessly drive growth in the ability and the desire to do whatever it takes for the good of the organization. Group wisdom and strength . . . the ability to ACT AS ONE, with a collective heartbeat . . . are the DNA elements enabling sustainable resilience. .

Creating Desire – On the Way to Group Wisdom and Strength

The basic question and the subject of this book is: How does an organization achieve group wisdom and strength, the ability to act as one, with a collective heartbeat? How does an organization build the ability and the desire to do whatever it takes for it to succeed easily, consistently, and sustainably? Wisdom and strength fuel ability and desire; they are iterative and symbiotic. Group wisdom and strength increase with each challenge overcome and each opportunity successfully seized. And as wisdom and strength increase, so do the ability and desire to meet new challenges and opportunities.

Knowledge grows from the availability of useful information (as opposed to raw data) and with guided experience (not memorized tasks). Trust evolves from involvement, openness and transparency, and shared values. It is the opposite of fear, which stifles sound thinking and judgment. Trust fosters independent thinking, encourages action and leads to more coordinated movement.

Resilience and sustainable growth are built from the core; they can't be achieved with superficial changes. **Communication** is the conductive gel that connects and melds pieces to grow **Knowledge** and **Trust**, layer by layer, strengthening the organization, building group wisdom and strength and enabling greater and greater resilience. With each problem that is solved or new opportunity that is seized and accomplished, the organization's core will become stronger. The culture becomes one of building knowledge and trust, which strengthens confidence and builds motivation (aka desire). With these embedded in the organization, it no longer depends on selected individuals to supervise and manage performance. New personnel learn this culture from others. Supervisors, managers and leaders have more time to perform at their highest levels of creativity, inspiration and development of themselves and others. Functioning with a collective heartbeat becomes part of the organization's DNA.

Ability Grounds Desire and Sustains It

Working together against adversity, whether on small problems or major challenges, using effective communication and good tools builds strength to the core. It is a circular process: Successful, consistent, team accomplishment will build individual *Knowledge* and *Trust* that, in turn, will grow into group strength and wisdom. The result is sustainable high performance and resilience (see Figure I.1).

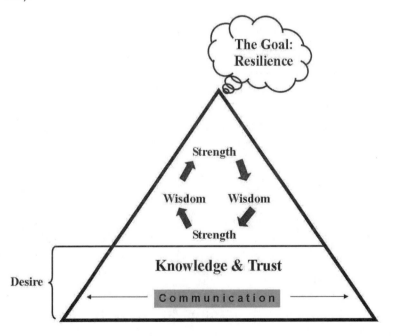

Figure I.1

Teams built this way easily and quickly impart *Knowledge* and *Trust* to new members. Those attributes cannot be built in an environment that relies on memorized tasks/duties that frequently don't make sense and require long waits for dictums that filter down through a bureaucratic pyramid.

Knowledge and Trust that enable *Resilience* are built on truly *understanding* the Vision, processes and purpose of each task and its link to the tasks of others and of the entire organization. That's just what happened in the Oregon Ducks' difficult game against Arizona, two games after the game that finally gave them the #1 ranking in 2010 and that clinched their berth in the BCS Championship Game that year. The Arizona game could have cost UofO the opportunity to play at that level.

Oregon was behind at the end of the half, 19 to 14. A freshman was playing in a significant role that night due to an injury a major player had received in the California game two weeks earlier. Another key playmaker was recovering from a collision in the first half, so in the second play of the second half, the ball was thrown to the freshman. He zigzagged a couple times and outran two fast Arizona players for 85 yards to make the touchdown. Only two runs in Oregon history were longer, one in 1938 and one in 2007. That complex run was a game-changer and the Ducks won, 48-29. The play was a new one, tried only once before, and it didn't quite work the first time, but the freshman tried it again when he knew something special was needed.[6] He knew he had his team behind him, took the risk and provided a spark when the team needed it most. He had already learned and internalized, even as a freshman, the keys to his team's success and trusted himself and his team. And his team trusted him.

This situation reminds me of my first rule for resilience:

Resilience Rule #1:
Plan B Doesn't Work

Learning many alternatives, which comes from knowing the systems and processes and with experience, is critical to good performance. But spending time developing a specific, detailed Plan B is wasted effort. Worse, like having a foot in two boats invites disaster, Plan B invites negative thinking and distracts from full attention and positive thinking about Plan A. Additionally, the exact situation in which a Plan B might be useful is never quite as it was imagined; real-time planning and creativity is needed in any case.

It is more effective and far more efficient to retrofit and create, when the situation presents itself, with a team that is well-informed, knows and trusts each other to the core, has proven judgment and is capable of quick thinking and acting. In other words, what is needed is a team that is resilient in the face of inevitable and continual challenges and changes. Then a great Plan B can be created when it's needed, efficiently and effectively.

As George Schultz says through the inimitable Charlie Brown, "The minute you start talking about what you are going to do if you lose, you have lost."

Desire & Ability – The Pillars of Resilience

Three core components: Strategic Planning (big picture, large scale view), effective Tools (structures, systems and processes) and Human Development, all linked, supported and built with effective Communication, create the *Ability* to respond to any challenges and accomplish goals consistently and successfully (see *Figure I.2*).

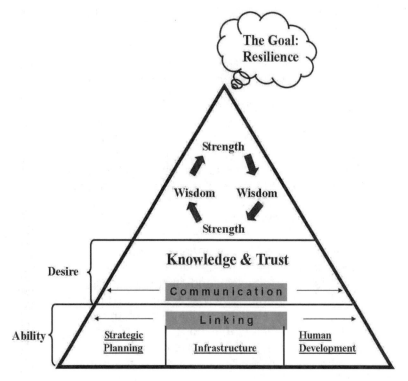

Figure I.2

But without the *Desire* to do whatever it takes for the good of the organization, resilience cannot occur. Ants have desire; they are born with it. Desire can also be developed the way 2010 NCAA Coach of the Year Chip Kelly did it, like Phil Knight and Bill Bowerman did. And like Clive Charles, legendary coach of tiny University of Portland's Women's Soccer team did when he led them from obscurity to the national championship game, again and again, playing against the biggest schools in the country.

When the Pilots won their second NCAA championship two years after the death of Clive Charles, author Brian Doyle wrote in *Portland Magazine:*

"It was the *way* they played...the camaraderie and creativity and coherence and generosity and quicksilver flow of their game as they bent it to their remarkable wills...

"Anyone who saw them flying through the riveting fall will never forget them, and there will always be Christine Sinclair...and coach Garrett Smith watching silently with his legs crossed, idly eating candy, as calm as a man waiting for a faraway train."[7]

Ability and **Desire**: Those two pillars support organizational Wisdom and Strength. Wisdom and strength, in turn, sustain the ability to *act with a Collective Heartbeat* — the DNA of Resilience (see Figure I-2). Indomitable teams, companies and ant colonies all achieve consistent success by building group wisdom and core strength that enable them, no matter the obstacle, to ***act with a Collective Heartbeat***. And that is how other organizations can build *Resilience DNA.*

PART 1 – DESIRE

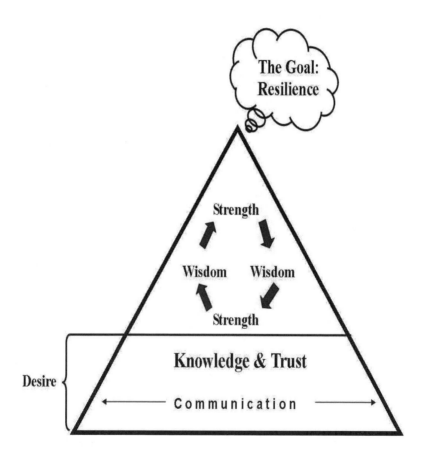

Chapter 1:
Common Knowledge
Capitalizing on Shared Experiences and Information

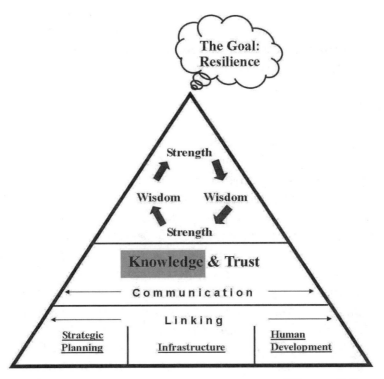

Figure 1.1

15

W ithout constant change, an organism will inevitably wither and die, whether the organism is a simple amoeba or a complex, multi-national corporation. But change can be wonderful or it can kill. What helps to assure that change is good and that it will happen successfully, expeditiously and constantly?

It doesn't matter how strong the management team or CEO is if they don't sufficiently use their individual strengths and wisdom to assure that the entire organization functions as a unified team, with a *collective heartbeat*. A major step is to assure expansive, integrated, open communication that propels team unity and amplifies the benefits of individual knowledge. Team unity speeds up progress and assures quality.

Let's take a look at ConArm, a co-op insurance company for the construction industry:

ConArm, Part 1
ConArm contracted out their Claims process to Jive, Inc., for twelve years. Jive's genius CEO and highly skilled claims adjusters were adept at customer relations. But with recent rapid growth, Jive developed severe internal operating deficiencies. The financial management and internal- and quality-control processes did not adequately support Jive's volume. Frequent transaction errors and slow payment of claims threatened success. ConArm then considered establishing their own Claims division, but instead, they successfully negotiated the acquisition of Jive.

For months, key managers at both companies met to discuss current customer issues, collaboration to obtain new customers, integration and transition of software systems, personnel changes, and marketing messages. Acquisition documents were signed, customers notified, new brochures and marketing materials ordered. The problem: Two days before 'going live,' someone realized that claims payments were ready to be issued but the new bank account was not opened and there was no check stock. The check approval and signing process was not established; internal controls for the payment process were not designed. Why?

ConArm's Accounting Department was not part of either the acquisition or subsequent implementation discussions. Accounting processes were considered secondary in the planning discussions and forgotten in the rush to implement the claims process changes. Accounting Department members knew about the acquisition and offered to participate in planning, but they were brushed off as unnecessary.

Change Distrust to Group Wisdom and Strength

Wisdom and Strength are core attributes; they must be intertwined to achieve success. Wisdom and Strength concepts apply to every CEO, every manager, every team, and every governmental and private organization and are basic to all organisms. An organization may have strength, evidenced by market dominance, talented leaders, and bullet-proof patents, but it won't stay strong very long if there isn't an effective way to continually collect and share knowledge and experience throughout to build and maintain group wisdom.

Consider the example of new information about competitor advances and how customers use the product or service. Individuals within organizations constantly receive this information, but its benefit is minimized for two reasons:

1. It is not shared sufficiently with people and departments throughout the organization.

2. Those who do receive the information don't have enough background knowledge to fully understand or effectively apply the knowledge to their work.

In contrast, when individuals receive adequate job training and when information about events and changes is passed down to all employees, the accumulated strength and wisdom assures that the new information will be used effectively throughout the organization.

An organization is able to obtain and maintain the essential traits of Strength and Wisdom by building the capacity to act in unity, as one, with a collective heartbeat — which enables Resilience — as illustrated in *Figure 1.1*. This is a circular process, as we will see in all the chapters of this book.

How is an organization able to accomplish this? Through individual and group knowledge and trust.

Knowledge and Trust Expand Motivation and Confidence

Individual knowledge, shared in an organizational environment that enables trust, leads to group Wisdom. Individual and group distrust, turned around by well-communicated information that is consistently proven to be true, soon transforms into group Trust. Individuals share their knowledge more openly with increasing trust, which leads to stronger group knowledge. Knowledge and Trust feed each other, delivering increased motivation and confidence with every positive occurrence.

Knowledge grows from absorbing useful information (not from data) and from reflecting on past experiences in applying information. Knowledge does not grow from performing memorized tasks. Conversely, organizations don't grow consistently and sustainably unless their people at all levels and in all departments grow in knowledge.

In addition, trust evolves from involvement, from repeated exposure to openness and transparency, and from recognition of shared values. Trust fosters independent thinking, encourages action and leads to more collaboration. In contrast, fear stifles sound thinking and judgment; it leads to paralysis and inaction.

An organization can perform with strength and wisdom only with the collective knowledge and the communal trust of its people. The only way to effectively access the collective knowledge of its people is by heightening the organization's ability to share. Unless the organizational TEAM can access the knowledge efficiently, acting as one, individual knowledge doesn't matter. Personnel who work with customers and vendors need to link effectively with the entire organization or their knowledge won't sufficiently benefit either the customer or the organization.

For example, the CEO and COO hear recommendations from an outside consultant about a planned new direction. They also hear an analysis of the situation, the rationale for and the benefits from the recommended steps, and a summary of how to implement the changes effectively. The CEO and COO, dealing directly with the consultant, probably discuss the alternatives, the pros and cons of each possible approach, the potential barriers and solutions, and the implications and applications of the recommended steps for the organization. They ask questions, voice concerns, and are reassured that their concerns were considered, or they request more research to resolve the concerns. Then, armed with their full understanding of the facts and conclusions, the CEO and

COO can wholeheartedly accept the suggestions and move confidently to lead their organization in the new direction.

Unfortunately, the CEO and COO don't usually replicate the entire scenario for anyone else in the organization. In most cases, they pass on only the recommendations and the directive to implement them. The CEO and COO may share selected pieces of the information they received but don't repeat the background and details that helped them to fully understand and agree on the plan. As a result of the inadequate sharing of background and the full decision-making process, other important partners and stakeholders probably will not fully embrace the proposed changes. They may see potentially detrimental implications for their department or for themselves that were already considered, debated and resolved, but because the detailed information leading to the conclusion was never shared, other stakeholders will continue to harbor doubts and misgivings.

Even more unfortunate, other stakeholders may see potentially detrimental implications for implementation not considered by the executives. The possible barriers and pitfalls could probably be easily resolved if the organization leaders knew about the issues. Instead of voicing their concerns, these stakeholders may voice support for the plan but then ignore or work against the change, fearing that it won't work or may be harmful, rather than work energetically to accomplish it. As problems and roadblocks emerge and push-backs inevitably erupt, the executives will probably share more about the alternatives and issues they considered. By then, there is already damage; the level of trust and honesty within the organization and the level of confidence in the leadership has dropped.

Managers frequently blame the employees for not buying into the change and for being the cause of the resulting problems. As a result, progress slows on the project due to little enthusiasm or motivation to make the new approach, acquisition, or new product roll-out work. More about this potential problem and solutions will be discussed in *Chapter 3 – The New Art of War.*

Figure 1.2 displays the typical huge reduction in knowledge that occurs when leaders work with outside resources on organizational problems or opportunities. The reduced flow of information not only minimizes the beneficial impact of the outside resource knowledge-sharing but it also leads to unnecessary mistakes and to subsequent second-guessing and distrust of leaders. The result of the improvement project or change plan is a reduction, rather than increase, in unifying the organization and its resilience.

Inadequate Sharing Stifles Innovation and Hampers Growth

It doesn't matter how much information a person or group receives; if it doesn't *effectively* go beyond that person or group, it has minimal value. Individuals must share their information in order to help build group knowledge and organizational Wisdom. Unless information is shared — including full descriptions and ways of applying it to real and hypothetical situations — there is no beneficial impact on the actions of other stakeholders who have a role in implementing, designing, or guiding team members. Worse yet, avoidable problems and mistakes slow or derail implementation because information wasn't communicated. The result is that some stakeholders unintentionally undermine the change. Needless damage occurs.

Reduced flow of information from outside Vendors, Consultants and Customers as it moves through the typical Organization

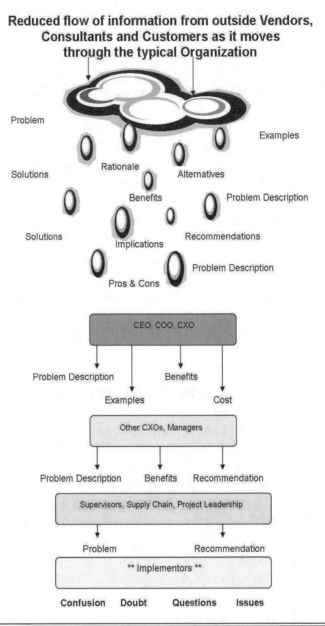

Figure 1.2

This destructive cycle happens far too frequently in most organizations, especially in larger, older, more-bureaucratic ones. The organization becomes more inefficient, less customer-focused and more change-averse with every attempted change effort.

The same problem develops when an executive guides or collaborates with a key internal manager to accomplish a new organization strategy or a new product application. Many managers or supervisors do not effectively share the guidance and plans they receive with their direct reports for many reasons, including time pressures, a desire to maintain control, or because they believe it will be more efficient to withhold the information.

Managers/supervisors may not understand that when their information isn't *effectively* linked with others, it will probably not accomplish the desired result. At a minimum, the project or task will take longer to accomplish and probably cause damage to their relationship with their staff. In many organizations, this situation is too frequently the norm. People withhold information in order to retain an advantage or because they believe the other person or group "doesn't need to know."

Inadequate sharing has a different, but often far greater, negative impact when it happens at the highest executive levels. Research, assessment, and findings of outside advisors may not be shared adequately with key executives. This lack of sharing reduces the beneficial impact of outside work and often exacerbates a negative, self-protective, selfish environment. For new knowledge to be used effectively, it should be shared completely with all key players. Equally important, services provided by key outside advisers have much greater impact and benefit to the organization if executives also have access to their knowledge and findings.

Deeper into the organization, inadequate sharing of information has a much more pervasive effect. For example, COOs have access to many evolving pieces of knowledge from outside and from across the organization, which is meaningful to work being done throughout. COOs may decide not to share some knowledge with supervisors or with other managers because they want to direct the changes and do not want anyone getting ahead of them (or getting credit for the change without them). So they withhold information until they believe the time is "right." This happens frequently as leaders seek to improve their reputations and positions.

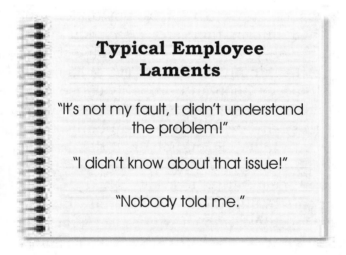

Typical Employee Laments

"It's not my fault, I didn't understand the problem!"

"I didn't know about that issue!"

"Nobody told me."

Most leaders may not realize that to accomplish almost any change successfully, the whole team must function as a unit. When the inevitable problem or failure occurs, the managers will be faulted and then seek causes outside of themselves for the less-than-total success. Unfortunately, managers frequently do not realize that it is within their own power to assure success simply through greater and earlier sharing of information.

Shared Knowledge Rule #1:
Fog Causes Accidents – on the Road
and in the Organization

People must understand the context before they can fully embrace and use knowledge. They must "see" the situation, to know the road, so they can react quickly and well to unforeseen situations. Just telling people what you think they 'need to know' to do their job isn't enough. Just giving them the "how to" instructions and steps that apply to their department or job won't result in effective implementation and adaptation. Without adequate and timely knowledge, people will make unnecessary mistakes or will need to return to their leaders for guidance instead of quickly and effectively responding to the issue themselves.

People must know the road and the plan as much as possible. They must understand the big picture, the timeline, the major goals, the other players and their roles, the potential problems. With that background, when different situations or new problems arise, workers at all levels will have sufficient knowledge to see the most likely pitfalls and compensate for them in advance. With full knowledge, they will be able to adapt the instructions and reconfigure processes to quickly solve unforeseen problems when they erupt, as they inevitably will.

Inadequate Information Sharing Leads to Costly Mistakes and Reduces Successful Results

When knowledge is not shared with all potentially affected departments, there is an even greater negative impact on the change project and also on the organization's resilience. Unshared information detracts from any department's ability to participate meaningfully in the planned change. Worse, when departments aren't fully involved or informed they aren't able to perform at the level or speed of other departments. Not knowing the cause but aware of their slow progress and experiencing frustration, uninformed managers and their key staff lose trust in the process and in their leaders. They lose their motivation, reduce their efforts, and "bad mouth" the project.

ConArm, Part 2

In the ConArm story that began this chapter, the Accounting Department was not invited to participate in the Jive acquisition planning or in the merged operations discussions. Other key operating executives considered the accounting process and system issues of secondary importance. The operating directors believed that they had enough knowledge of relevant accounting issues and implications without bogging down deliberations with "details." Because their attempts to participate were rebuffed and they were not able to voice their concerns about potential issues, accounting personnel began hinting to other departments that there would be problems with execution of the merger plans.

The Accounting Department was initially blamed for not setting up the claims account and for not ordering the checks. Accounting personnel reacted. They protested that they were not involved in any of the planning for Jive, despite their offers of help.

26

They were not aware of the new structure and didn't know the process for integrating transactions or how payments would be handled. Everyone believed that Accounting was an after-the-fact player and didn't need to be involved in the planning stage.

When knowledge isn't shared, the potential for creativity in seeing possible problems and opportunities from all organizational perspectives is lost. Worse yet, employees who might be energized and reinforced in their desire to add value to the organization feel disenfranchised and ignored. They can't help without full knowledge of the big picture and the specific situation. Organizations diminish their potential for resilience with every problem solved or new opportunity that is addressed without adequate information-sharing.

The *ConArm* merger problem is an example of why an attitude and culture of real *knowledge-sharing* is so critical to successful change, as opposed to simply delivering directives and implementation instructions when and if it is *perceived* to be needed by others.

Every change project is an opportunity for enhancing resilience within the organization's DNA. The opportunity is lost without effective sharing during the change process.

"It is not simply that we share with each other a common humanity, but that individually we have no humanity without each other."

— *Sara Maitland*

27

Shared Knowledge Rule #2: Take Time Upfront or Lose It in the Crunch!

When preparing to implement new initiatives, if you don't provide the full picture and engage in discussions about the application, alternatives, and possible implications at the earliest stages, you will lose huge amounts of time when you need it most. Even worse, you will jeopardize the organization's ability to build a culture of continuous improvement and innovation.

When introducing new technology, new product or service designs and new processes, people in selected departments usually receive only limited information: the functions and applications that apply to their immediate jobs. The orientation doesn't typically include the background history (the 'why'), how it will be utilized by other departments, and how that connects to their work. They don't receive sufficient information about the alternatives researched, why the solution was selected, and its benefits in contrast to alternative solutions. People are not provided meaningful opportunities to ask their questions about alternatives or implications or to voice their concerns about implementation issues and the application of the change to specific situations.

With adequate contextual information and sufficient opportunities for real discussion, all personnel will have the background to research and develop creative approaches to solve problems or approach new opportunities expeditiously on their own.

Here's an example of what happens when implementation groups compete with one another and withhold information as a competitive tactic. The result is inadequate sharing, which hurts both groups and the company.

Acrobat Instruments, Part 1

Acrobat Instruments was a small, rapidly growing manufacturer with an exciting product. Acrobat hired two small marketing firms to work on related projects. Each firm had a fabulous reputation in its specialty niche — one with public relations, the other with advertising — although they both also offered services in the other's specialty niche. Although each firm preferred to do the entire project, the client wanted each firm's superior niche skill — the best marketing minds and reputations Acrobat could hire.

The Challenge: *Producing a great result in two separate but intertwined service areas is possible, but it requires close collaboration. If the exemplary skills were in one firm, good communication and knowledge-sharing would be simpler. When two firms see each other as competitors, the challenge is greater. The difficulty in utilizing highly skilled, self-confident groups with overlapping expertise is the natural tendency for each to want to do it all and not want to share lest the other use their ideas and get credit or "botch" the project. The fear factor grows and negatively affects collaboration and, therefore, the potential for a successful project. This also occurs frequently with competing divisions or siloed departments. Acrobat was aware of this risk but knew that neither firm would agree to be managed by the other. The alternative approach was for Acrobat to manage both marketing firms and integrate their activities through good communications processes.*

It didn't work.

The firms went around Acrobat; they jockeyed for position — similar to what happens when groups compete within an organization.

Distrust, caused by lack of knowledge of the role, working processes and best skills of the other firm, and fear that the other firm might usurp part of their role, inhibited the firms' ability to act in unity for the good of the project.

The result is the same when teams within an organization don't have adequate knowledge of the other teams. They act out of underlying distrust and fear; the result is less-than-optimum success for the organization or for either team. While appearing to work together, they jockey for position and undermine the actions of the other department or team. They justify their actions because they truly believe the other organization or team doesn't have the skills or the best interest of the company as their primary motivation.

In Acrobat's case, one firm walked away, leaving the other firm and the client company to complete the project. The project was completed, but both firms lost the potential for beneficial collaborations in the future. They might have built an important alliance to enable them to work on large projects that neither one could handle independently. The project ended with some very good products for Acrobat, but the two firms and Acrobat lost the exciting, on-going development and breakthrough results that could have occurred with greater knowledge-sharing and subsequent linking.

Although this example was with two firms that could opt to walk away rather than work to fix the distrust and fear issues, the same situation occurs within organizations to the detriment of the project. Each time an issue or new project develops, if the opportunity is not used to build shared knowledge and trust — to build greater unity — the underlying problems within the organization become more embedded in the culture.

True Sharing of Information/Knowledge
Knowledge sharing and truly collaborating as a unified team — *with a collective heartbeat* — is the most important concept for organizational success. Organizational Strength and Wisdom can be built and used to major advantage only with effective knowledge-sharing. People are empowered to make changes and proactively make improvements when they receive:

- Sufficient Knowledge — for complete information

- Adequate Tools — to enable information-sharing

- Effective Access — to knowledge resources and information tools

Developers and users of Knowledge Management systems must focus more on the access to and breadth of information-sharing to all stakeholders: the user-friendliness of the resources. Knowledge Management systems are wonderful *tools* that help to link individuals and teams through sharing knowledge across the organization.[1,2]
The most common complaint within organizations that have these valuable systems is that the systems are not utilized sufficiently to maximize their benefits and justify their cost. The problem is

that most organizations don't have an environment that supports true collaboration and desire to share information. Without a more unified environment, there is little motivation or commitment to consistently use or expand the knowledge systems.

Shared Knowledge Rule #3 – Without an Environment that Promotes Knowledge Sharing, Information Will Be Used to Damage or Destroy

Information is the most powerful tool for influencing the pace and sustainability of change. It can foster, facilitate, expedite and assure the sustainability of change.

Fear is the inhibitor of change. Fear can be fed or assuaged – with information. Information can be used to sabotage change. Examples surround us – political campaigns, environmental issues, healthcare issues, wherever there is potential for change. Information is a powerful tool that can be used by negative forces to manipulate, distort or amplify negatives to fight change.

Information is frequently used to distort or destroy; we have all seen that happen with governmental entities. Information is most insidiously misused in rural areas because a small population is more easily manipulated. *Wood County* leaders learned that honest, transparent, well-researched, widely-shared knowledge effectively counters misinformation.

Wood County, Part 1
Wood County, remote and rural, in gorgeous high-desert country with deep canyons and pristine rivers, had deep economic problems, brought on by

the increasing number of laws to protect national forests from logging. Major timber and forest product companies closed; unemployment increased in Wood County while economic health increased in other counties within the state. The economic development department of the state offered funding and expert resources to help to build new industries in these distressed counties.

The nine incorporated towns in the County all vied for state and federal grants. Each town had its own plans for attracting business and tourists to its community. Collectively, their grant requests were much more than the funds available to this small population area. The state's offer to the towns: Work together to develop a collaborative strategic plan for development of the County's economy.

The Problem: *Traditional competition among the small towns, now compounded by their economic situation, was heightened further by the fear that their individual town plans would be diminished by the plans of other communities. Additionally, in each town, distrust of the county government in the face of reduced budgets for programs led citizens to accusations of favoritism, second-guessing motives, and finger-pointing, especially at the elected county and city leaders. Several leaders faced recall and lost their positions. Many others, including the current county judge (chair of the county commission), were threatened with recall. Fear prevailed in this county, fueled by the loud, negative and distorted messages of very active dissidents.*

The Judge was frequently driven by fear, afraid to make significant decisions. He believed that bringing representatives from each town together to begin working on a joint Strategic Plan, with the project paid for by "Big Brother" state government, would lead to recall efforts.

This kind of fear, further discussed in *Chapter 3 — The New Art of War*, is rampant in organizations throughout the world today. Everyone is afraid of making mistakes, so they no longer take the personal risks that lead to beneficial change, and, in turn, to innovation and improvement.

International consultant Eric Garland described the death of Strategic Planning in organizations. He researched and documented the root cause of the inhibiting fear as the need today to take safe positions unless you know everyone is behind you. This self-protective reaction drives people to act from conventional wisdom and with a risk-avoidance perspective. This reaction is increasingly prevalent because of the social media enabled power of individuals to mass-distribute their thoughts and perceptions, whether accurate or not. The vacuum of inadequate knowledge creates a breeding ground for misinformation.[3]

The only counter-strategy to negative information for leaders is transparency and lots of sound, accurate information as *early* as possible, rather than waiting until something negative happens.

The Solution to Fear-Induced Inaction

As Sun Tzu, the inspired Chinese general and author of *The Art of War*, wrote 2500 years ago:

> "If you know the enemy and know yourself, you need not fear the result of a hundred battles. If you know yourself but not the enemy, for every victory gained you will also suffer a defeat. If you know neither the enemy nor yourself, you will succumb in every battle."

Sun Tzu believed that knowledge of self (the individual and the organization) is the starting point for any victory.[4] His philosophies are still required reading in many Asian cultures, even in grade schools, because of their application to daily work and even to social interaction.

Dr. Daniel Goleman and his team of Harvard researchers proved that the awareness of self and of others and the ability to control self and influence others is the key differentiator for achieving success in today's complex organizations. Their landmark research resulted in the concept of Emotional Intelligence.[5,6]

Good leaders foster dissemination and sharing of knowledge in their organizations by:

1. Working to assure an environment that fosters openness and transparency

2. Promoting and supporting the development of information-sharing tools

3. Being an advocate and promoter of meaningful, digestible, and adaptable information (not data)

Knowledge-Sharing and Linking
Partnering firms and internal teams alike lose two major potential benefits if they don't effectively link and share information with one another. They can't optimally benefit the organization.

The strengths of any team can't be effectively utilized if team members don't individually and collectively understand as much as possible about the organization's current plans, activities, abilities and weaknesses. This information can be learned only through effective sharing and linking with other teams.

Chapter 2:
Chemistry 101
Linking the Organization through Shared Values and Transparency

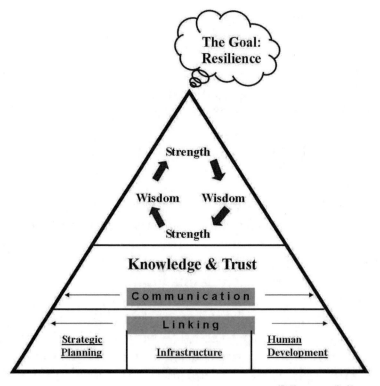

Figure 2.1

Dahlstrom Inner-City League, Part 1

Dahlstrom Inner-City League was an exciting organization with an innovative approach to helping the homeless. The founder, a gifted and technically knowledgeable professional with great contacts in their industry, chose a Board of Directors of talented medical and social scientists and inner-city business people with links to funding sources.

As Dahlstrom gained visibility, the role of the Board of Directors became more important; they needed to know the status and plans for operations, finance, marketing, and funding. The founder/CEO began sending detailed charts, graphs, historical data, and 50-page financial and transaction reports, all revised continually, sometimes weekly. Board members were inundated with information they couldn't comprehend, that frequently wasn't applicable to their roles, and that they didn't have the time (or desire) to read.

Board meetings became dog-and-pony shows, led by the founder, that didn't invite participation and discussion. Board members began to skip meetings and, when they did come, they were unprepared. Their involvement in Dahlstrom diminished just as their knowledge, skills and connections were most needed. It was evident to the Board members that their ideas and input were not valued.

Dahlstrom is an example of what happens when stakeholders are not truly involved in the what, why, and how of an organization's activities. They stop believing in the organization; they lose what interest they might have had. They lose *trust* in the leaders, in the organization's ability to accomplish its goals. They lose their desire to be connected to the organization. With employees, this becomes dis-interest: "It's just a job." With Board members and volunteers, and with constituents of governmental entities, it leads to disinterest and disengagement.

Trust fosters independent thinking, encourages action and leads to greater commitment to the organization. Trust grows with involvement, in an environment of openness and transparency, and with commonly shared values.

- *Involvement* is more than just working together on tasks. It is meaningful participation in planning, development, and decision-making.

- People believe in the *openness and transparency* of the organization and its leaders when they consistently receive useful information and experience repeated incidents that confirm the validity of the information.

- *Shared values* develop and are strengthened as people concurrently encounter issues and work together to resolve them.

Involvement, openness and transparency, and shared values — essential to building Trust and commitment — all grow in an environment where collaboration is valued and promoted.

The Linking Concept – Collaboration

The more personal wisdom and strength that individuals have, the greater their ability to effectively collaborate. On the flip side, collaboration leads to stronger links and relationships among individuals and groups; it therefore promotes the building of

organizational wisdom and strength. It is an iterative process — Wisdom and Strength are needed for
successful collaboration and also increase as a
result of it. Leaders can begin the iterative process
to building *true* collaboration with a commitment to
effective communication of honest, complete and
useful information. Communication includes both
processes and *tools* to facilitate the exchange of
knowledge and building of trust (see *Figure 2.1* on
page 35).

Effective communication processes and tools
(systems), along with the following organizational
attributes, enable collaboration:

- Organization values are always visible and
  consistently reinforced at all levels.

- Processes are in place to take information
  from core relationships — customers and
  vendors — upwards to the top level leaders.

- The communication process is sustainable —
  so everyone can keep communicating at these
  levels, no matter what — ensuring that all
  employees continue receiving useable information, tools and access whenever needed.

These three positive attributes enable people to
share information and experiences, collaboratively
building group knowledge into teams consistently
acting with a collective heartbeat.

Leaders at the middle of the organization are the
interpreters (see *Figure 2.2*). Mid-level managers
and supervisors are the most critical but frequently
undervalued people in the communications
process. Their access to detailed knowledge and
their subsequent detailed sharing of that knowledge

The Critical Role of Mid-Managers and Supervisors in the Vertical Flow of Knowledge

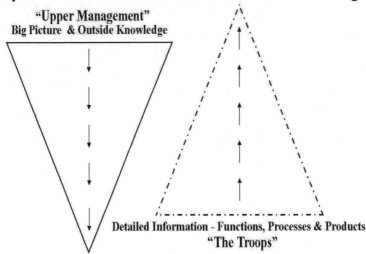

"Upper Management"
Big Picture & Outside Knowledge

Detailed Information - Functions, Processes & Products
"The Troops"

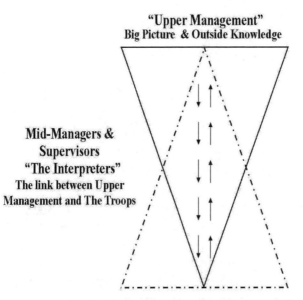

"Upper Management"
Big Picture & Outside Knowledge

Mid-Managers &
Supervisors
"The Interpreters"
The link between Upper
Management and The Troops

Detailed Information - Functions, Processes & Products
"The Troops"

Figure 2.2

can make or break any planned strategy. Their open and complete exchange of information up, down and across the organization is paramount in assuring that successful collaboration can occur.

Many organizations understand the necessity for good flow of information *across* the organization (cross-channel communication) but they don't do it effectively, either. *Chapter 5 — Process Power* will discuss methods for achieving real communication (involvement) *horizontally*.

The Acrobat situation in *Chapter 1 — Common Knowledge*, gives us a third example of frequently undervalued knowledge exchange. Acrobat's story highlights the need to provide detailed information about the recommendations of *outside* advisors/ vendors to other advisors and to the people within Acrobat.

When working with outside resources, linking and collaboration should occur in at least three directions so that internal groups can effectively develop and implement the recommendations:

1. between each outside firm and the organization's leaders

2. among outside resources

3. throughout the organization

Typically, the focus of communication is only on 1 and partially on 3. Steps 2 and 3 usually get short shrift — only minimal, if any, attention. The beneficial users of the information, both internal and external, are the last to know.

Insufficient knowledge-sharing by individuals reduces group knowledge. This then reduces the organization's capacity for optimum collaboration.

As a result, the potential for sustainable project success is also inadvertently *reduced.* In the long run, the change will not work!

To maximize the potential for successful change, the communication process should simultaneously work in reverse to collect information from internal teams at all levels about the implications of the proposed changes, and as they work to implement changes, to share with organization leaders and representatives from the advisor or vendor firms. The communication process should be iterative and expanding, with changing teams and changing roles as the project progresses, always seeking wider and stronger circles of involvement and awareness.

Linked Organization Rule #1:
Linking Enhances Creativity

As two-way exchanges of information occur with increasing depth and breadth, leaders hear more about the impact and get a more detailed view of the project. All levels understand more about current and potential issues.

Expanded knowledge leads to greater awareness and new creative thought that benefit high-level decision-making and amplify use of the project's products at all levels and spans of the organization, even while project implementation is still underway. *Chapter 8 – People Focus*, explains this in more detail.

Make Information Useable!

Besides not communicating broadly and deeply enough, organizations typically have another communication problem that inhibits their ability to build strong teams, sustain changes and achieve organization resilience: They don't present information in a way that promotes understanding by the intended audience. Information may not be useable because it wasn't developed with a focus on user needs or designed in an inviting, easily readable and understandable format.

Communication processes and *information systems* ensure that information will be useable and, therefore, help to achieve effective collaboration.

Communication processes should be designed using multiple teams and individuals to represent various perspectives, issues, and needs within the organization. The teams should determine:

• What information is needed

• From what sources

• Using which technology systems

• To whom it should be distributed

• How often

• What communication vehicles/tools to use

Many good *Information Systems* and methods are available to help individuals collect, format, analyze, manipulate, interpret, summarize and disseminate information to all teams as needed. For example, see Knowledge Management systems in *Chapter 1 — Common Knowledge.*

As information is distributed, communication processes and information systems can also be used to collect and share reactions, insights, and suggested improvements from both the organization and from outside contractors and vendors. This expanded input enables more collaboration in the future (see *Figure 2.3*). Although electronic systems are useful in collecting and disseminating information, in-person processes are equally important to achieve major synergy benefits of shared knowledge (see *Chapter 4 – Real Involvement*).

Hierarchy of Communication Levels, Tools and Attributes for Achieving Group Knowledge

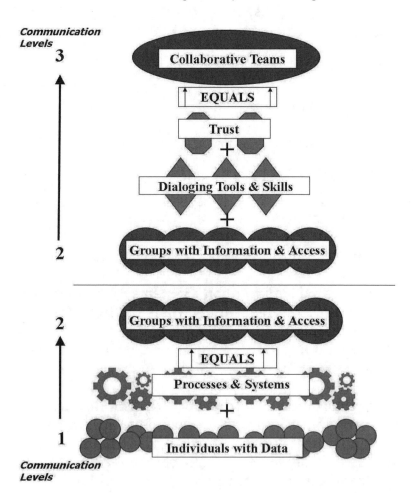

Figure 2.3

How You Do It Matters!

Both verbal and written communication must be effective for the process to achieve desired results. As everyone has experienced, just because meetings are held or memos are written does not mean that there will be good communication and sharing. Similarly, just because data is documented and distributed does not mean that useful information or knowledge is shared. Today's cryptic texts and emails make the possibility of real information sharing even more problematic.

This process area — exchange of information and individual knowledge — is where most organizations damage their own change efforts. They do not achieve effective sharing.

How you do it always matters!

Ineffective preparation and process undermine potential for *true* collaboration, so most entities never achieve substantial Wisdom and Strength.

You *can* achieve effective communication by strengthening these attributes:

1. **Adequate sharing level** — Are proactive methods used to find out *who* needs information — across the organization and at all levels? Without access to adequate sharing mechanisms, individuals use their personal perceptions to decide what to share and with whom. When mistakes occur due to lack of information, resentments build, complaints mushroom. Background information that should have explained the issue in advance (rationale, alternatives, big-picture perspective, and trouble-shooting processes) drizzles out on an ad hoc basis to those who complain or suffer the most. Meanwhile, hidden under the surface, other problems develop.

2. **Awareness of needs and frequent feedback** — Does the organization have adequate processes and protocols for determining *what* information needs to be shared — for both technical and general purpose information? When problems develop, does the organization fully assess the root cause or does it just react to the most-visible, most-immediate symptom? Does it proactively assess, across a broad spectrum, whether information needs are being met instead of waiting for problems (personnel, customer, or product quality) to develop?

3. **Useable information formats** (presentation methods and levels) — Does the organization involve representative users to design and assess the *format* for presenting information to ensure that it will be utilized, effectively understood and interpreted by all groups that need it? Or does someone in IT or another designated department design the format assuming that all departments will understand and be able to use the information and that all departments have the same needs? Information that doesn't specifically meet individual needs causes unnecessary mistakes and wastes huge amounts of time in interpretation and modification. Or worse, it is completely ignored. Useless or inadequate information also has a negative side-effect: It creates resentments and distrust of other departments and organization leaders.

4. **Attractive and useful information delivery vehicles** — Do representatives from various sectors of your organization assess the best

information delivery methods? The increasing variety of information delivery vehicles (print, audio, electronic, in person) provides the ability to select the most effective method based on the individual who will receive and use the information. Different methods are more effective depending upon the industry or the company, but also consider what will be more effective at different levels or in different areas within your organization.

The 2012 U.S. presidential election was the hottest, closest one ever. Advances in technology allowed pollsters to compare and assess the effectiveness of communication vehicles for the first time. This election, the most expensive because of a huge increase in polling, used electronic analysis throughout the campaign. This analysis showed that the most effective solution for reaching and engaging people was the old-fashioned way: Personal calls were more effective than computer-generated calls and personal (front door) visits were more effective than phone calls.

Misty Woods, Inc., Part 1

Inadequate sharing of information almost derailed this rapidly growing, otherwise healthy company:

Misty Woods, a rural health services provider that contracts with State and rural government entities, was experiencing exponential growth but began encountering quality-control and customer-service issues. These issues threatened their reputation and their customer retention, as frequently occurs with rapidly growing organizations. At the center of the problem was their finance department. It was

responsible for internal information that all departments used for billing, potential customer proposals,
customer statements, sales and productivity reports,
product planning and financial reports. Reports were
not accurate, not timely or not complete — frequently
all three. Customer communications and service
quality at all departments suffered.

The problems had various contributing causes,
many of which went beyond the finance department.
A principal flaw was inadequate communication and
sharing across all departments and within the
finance department itself.

Common Misperception:

Linked Organization Rule #2:
Look at Finance First – It is the Hub!

Frequently, when there are structural or process issues
throughout an organization, the problems are most visible
within the finance/accounting departments. They typically
receive, assimilate, manipulate, summarize and then
distribute information to all departments. It is the principal
link and interpreter of information. For that reason, it
often appears that the finance or accounting department
is the cause of information-reporting problems. Problems
that surface in this department are almost always a
symptom of more pervasive problems.

An observer at Misty Woods' only regular cross-
department information-sharing event, the monthly
manager meeting, would see the first major clue to
the cause of the problem: There was little real
interchange of ideas. Each manager presented an
activity report, but there was no format for sharing
recent problems or upcoming needs so that other

departments could offer suggestions or ask about activities that might affect their departments. Major up-coming company challenges were outlined, like the planned merger, but since little information was distributed for advance reading, there were few questions and minimal discussion.

The lack of opportunities for substantive sharing across departments in real time, or even at the one monthly opportunity for communication, significantly contributed to all departments' inability to respond effectively to their internal and external customers. Inadequate information-sharing especially affected the Finance department's ability to anticipate and to respond to data recording and integration issues.

Improving the quality of communication across all departments, both daily and weekly, substantially improved the situation for Finance and other departments. Better-informed managers collaborated more; they had greater knowledge that enabled them to make continuous effective improvements in customer service and product quality.

Too much data, as we saw with the *Dahlstrom* example at the beginning of this chapter, causes similar problems. When leaders and administrators disseminate information to their stakeholders, they should always design it with the goal of facilitating communication and achieving true collaboration. Just because meeting summaries and the related materials are distributed does not mean that they will be read, understood and acted upon.

The ability to use the *collective, unified* Wisdom and Strength of both leaders and key stakeholders depends upon effective organization processes, with the appropriate people involved, who understand the issues and who are able to fully participate and interact — true collaboration.

You can proactively build organizational Wisdom and Strength through:

- **Empowered teams** with full information and access to expertise, whose opinion is openly and frequently sought.

- **True collaboration** enabled through frequent, effective communication processes and structures and through an environment that promotes true sharing.

- **Basic communication enhancers** — simplified, summarized information relevant to the user.

A Common Language, a Common Goal — The Professional Services Council (PSC)

The Plan: The Professional Services Council was formed to bring together six professions (attorneys, accountants, engineers, architects, marketing, public relations and advertising, and management consultants) to build a strong, nationally visible industry cluster for Oregon.

The Council members successfully completed the design and formation of the new organization. Representatives of firms, many of them hot competitors, worked together to build the infrastructure and to create professional programs that would foster solid working relationships across the professions and also enhance the high-level business savvy of the members and professionals in their firm.

A key project for the Council was development of cross-professional curriculum in collaboration with Oregon universities. Representatives from each profession built a pyramid with various levels of desired common-knowledge topics. The base of the pyramid was foundation skills, including learning and communication techniques and industry core knowledge, subjects currently delivered as standard university curriculum. The second pyramid level included basic business skills not usually offered by the industry-focused university departments/schools, such as customer service, project management, marketing, and finance. The top pyramid level included entrepreneurial and leadership knowledge areas.

The professionals agreed on a list of undergraduate courses in areas not currently offered by Oregon universities. The new courses would produce better-prepared graduates who could then become effective professionals more quickly and who would compare more favorably with their new hires from schools outside Oregon. The cost to develop new courses would be shared across departments and with the professional service firms who would provide both monetary and personnel resources.

The Challenge: *The next step was to locate a university that would agree to work on the project with highly regarded professionals from the best firms in the state. These professionals agreed to donate their time to collaborate with the professors in designing one selected course. As an incentive to the university, the firms agreed on the benefits they would offer: In addition to giving recruiting preference to the university, the firms also agreed to send their previous new hires to take the collaboratively developed course and also to expand their intern programs to involve more students and professors in work-study traded positions with their firms.*

In 1998, the collaboration concept was new and potentially valuable to all participants: the "partner" schools, the firms, and the students. In addition to the benefits offered by the firms, the project would probably generate national publicity and result in heightened national visibility for the university's professional programs and for Oregon.

The Result: *The first test course was completed, but then the project ended. The obvious reasons: 1) The universities didn't want to collaborate in developing curriculum with outside professionals, and 2) academics and outside professionals differed in their definitions of "collaboration." The underlying causes were two barriers to innovation that always diminish the potential for success in organizations, especially in large bureaucratic ones: 1) Each group's desire for control over every stage of the project, as opposed to true collaboration and 2) A strong risk-avoidance culture that stifles creativity.*

The University offered the new course as a capstone: for over twelve years, it was one of the most popular courses for students desiring careers in the six professions. But sadly, no additional courses were developed through a process that could have led to hugely beneficial, expanding relationships with leading private-sector firms and leaders. The reason: The idea of collaboration outside the normal sphere of intra-university partners was threatening rather than fulfilling for the academic professionals.

Development of the first course was successful because an enlightened university president saw potential for a new kind of partnership with private-sector specialists to aid in growing the university's departments/schools.

The president departed the university just as the project started. Without the innovative, risk-taking president to push, the provost, deans and professors balked at the process, which required additional time commitment by the academics involved (as well as by the outside professionals) outside their normal work periods.

Linked Organization Rule #3:
Agree on Definition of Key Terms

To accomplish breakthrough, sustainable gains, team members must develop a common definition of key terms. With PSC, the most important term was "collaboration."

The greatest challenge to the project was engaging a university that would work collaboratively with leading experts from professional service firms to develop curriculum. But working with anyone outside academia is a "sacred cow" issue in most universities. The competence and knowledge of "outsiders" doesn't matter. In this case, there was an unknown barrier to common definition.

To the educators, "collaboration" meant that academics would research, design, and write the course. Then, educators would present it to outside professionals for suggestions. Private-sector professionals view "collaboration" as first, joint brainstorming on research and design, followed by team assignments to draft content and combined group assessment, debate, and revision.

Control and ownership vs. working together as partners . . . These are very different concepts with very different results. In his landmark work on Systems Thinking, *The Fifth Discipline[1]*, Peter Senge described the impact of unrecognized differences in mental models. These basic mismatches in thinking frequently thwart team efforts to efficiently arrive at innovative, successful and sustainable solutions to problems. The key is to recognize, define, and work within these differing mental models.

With *true* collaboration, there are no limits to what can be accomplished — working together as partners, with agreed and changing roles, moving towards *Acting As One,* with a *collective heartbeat.*

First, Focus on the Individual

Bill Bowerman was the legendary coach of Steve Prefontaine and other great players. He coached, then partnered with, Phil Knight to found and build Nike. He is the most significant coach-to-mega-entrepreneur I know of. He learned and taught the basic concept of building great teams: Every player is different.[2] So is every organization. You can't train, coach, or assess everyone in the same way. It doesn't work. It isn't effective because each of us, individually and organizationally, is unique. But we need to use our individual talents, knowledge, and instincts together, with a *collective heartbeat*, to create and accomplish what we could not do simply as individuals working together superficially. We need to act *as one* when needed but to think individually for the good of the whole.

Coach Chip Kelly of the incredibly resilient 2011 University of Oregon football team gave a message to his troops that basically said the same thing. It was posted on their locker doors:

1. Have fun

2. Stick together

3. Eliminate distractions

4. Flip the switch[3]

It is *focus on the individual*, first and foremost, that builds resilient Teams. A consistent and predictable process that every individual understands, accepts, and, finally, *trusts* will empower him or her to take initiative and exercise informed judgment in solving organizational problems, creating greater efficiencies, and designing improved products and services.

Arbitrary or unreasonable demands, posturing, or one-way debates are ineffective in achieving long-term, sustainable change or resilient organizations. That approach does not build Trust.

Individual and team Knowledge must be built and continually communicated to all — knowledge of the organization, of the product/service, of the roles, and of the processes. Ants, known to be the most resilient of all species, are born with knowledge of the colony's roles and processes. They learn more from one another with their highly developed communication mechanisms as the anthill community grows and overcomes adversity. The Oregon Ducks built that individual and team knowledge through conditioning in only two years. Nike did it with skilled internal coaching as each challenge was encountered and overcome. The University of Portland Women's soccer team retained it year after year (with four former players on the 2011 World Cup teams), eight years after the death of beloved coach Clive Charles. "His former players said . . . he made you feel like you were the only person in the room . . ."[5] He developed the process for training and took the school to their first National Championship in 2002, the year of his death.

For resilience and sustainable strength, there must also be communication of underlying values and total transparency about the organization to achieve Trust. Trust builds unity and unity creates resilient teams. As one leader at the University of Portland told me, "The women soccer players have the essence of it. The men have the same coaches with the same wonderful skills, but they haven't communicated and developed within themselves the inner core of Trust and Unity and focus that the women have and continue to communicate, year after year."

Trust and unity are achieved only by reaching people individually, at their core and building from there. People benefit from having coaches, managers, and leaders with Emotional Intelligence[5,6] and the critical traits of strength and humility described in *Good to Great* by Jim Collins.[7]

Additionally, all supervisors and project leaders need core tools and skills to help others *act as ONE, with a collective heartbeat.* They need process-thinking tools and good communication processes to build an environment of Trust that will positively affect every person at every level. The best leaders recognize that they need to develop both their left- and right-brain capabilities in order to be effective. To learn more, read *A Whole New Mind* by Daniel H. Pink.[8]

In the Professional Services Council story, the test project was successfully completed, but the long-term, significant growth goal was not. The major linking project that would have benefited all stakeholders (including and especially the students) was not achieved.[9] The two groups, academics and outside professionals, could not truly collaborate. An insurmountable lack of trust caused the failure. True collaboration cannot occur without trust, and trust cannot be built without effective communication of knowledge.

Shared Values and Transparency – Linking to Achieve Collaboration

Effective information-sharing across organizations and involvement at all levels enables unification and the ability to work together effectively. The first step is to determine what people need and then provide that information openly to all who need it. This begins the iterative process to enable the level of trust that will spur each individual to share their knowledge and build greater group knowledge. Frequently, individuals ask themselves this question before sharing their knowledge: For what purpose will my knowledge be used?

To trigger the level of trust and desire needed for open, true collaboration, there must be buy-in to the values driving the organization. More about that in *Chapter 3 – The New Art of War.*

How does an organization assure that its values are communicated and delivered in a way that individuals can internalize them and be motivated by them? By building a structure and environment that supports and reinforces total transparency in sharing knowledge.

In many organizations, especially bureaucratic ones, the absence of trust totally derails projects and continually damages the environment. The result is little desire to take the personal or group risks necessary to achieve innovation and to attain new levels of organizational success. On the other, more beneficial hand, an environment of Trust enables individuals to take risks and to seek new, creative goals to achieve for both themselves and their organization.

Chapter 3:
The New Art of War

Empowering Individuals through Creating
an Environment of Trust

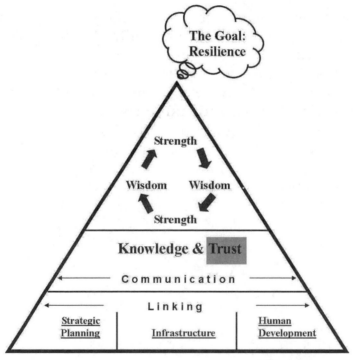

Figure 3.1

Crossbow Enterprises, Part 1

The Trust problem showed up early in the merger planning for three very visible not-for-profits. While membership was declining in each and all facilities needed improvement, members wanted more programs. Together, the organizations could accomplish their goals, but none could on their own. Merger into a new entity, Crossbow Enterprises, was critical.

I met with the CEOs to select member leaders for interviews. The interviews were important to collect information about the cultures, people and programs for an initial assessment of merger challenges and issues. The name of one of the most influential leaders, a respected attorney, came up, but the CEOs all agreed, "Don't talk to Ted. He's trying to derail the merger. He'll just use the interview to gather more information to work against it." I told them that Ted's concerns might help in learning what we needed to do in the planning process.

Ted was articulate and forceful in describing his opposition to the merger. I told him that the purpose of the interview was to understand his issues. I assured him that his input would help us to better assess the problems and develop better alternatives. Ted was obviously committed to the organizations.

He listened to reasons for the merger and the objectives for the combined future, which he hadn't understood before. I listened to all his issues. He was right; he had spotted flaws in the potential plan. I asked him to work with us. Ted said, "Thank you for listening. I will help to resolve these problems."

He agreed to chair a planning committee and, later, joined the merged Board of Directors. Because we listened, because we responded to his legitimate concerns, and because we involved him in planning and implementation, Ted helped immeasurably in accomplishing a successful merger.

Ted's fears for the planned merger were justified. There were many issues and challenges ahead. But his fears were reduced when he understood the organizations' current problems and the potential benefits of the merger. He was happy when he heard that there would be a well-structured planning and implementation process and that he and other capable members would be substantively involved. He embraced the merger.

There is no way to motivate people who aren't in the right frame of mind to be motivated. Urgings, pleas, even promises of good results won't work if people don't believe that the desired change will happen and benefit the company and their jobs. Embedded fears get in the way of belief.

What Causes Fear? How Does It Build?[1]
The world economy is in upheaval; major institutions (from churches to government and industry) are in crisis; and armed conflict, massive acts of terror, and natural disasters all affect the lives of individuals and the success of organizations.

Responding to all this turmoil creates MORE change and complexity. Fear incapacitates some people while others triumph from the opportunities that change creates.

What differentiates organizations that succeed from those that fail is their reaction to fear. Fear can disable us or it can spur us to creative action. The more frequently that people and organizations respond negatively to change, the more that negative reaction will be embedded in the culture and in the environment. The reverse concept is also true: The more that people and organizations practice positive responses to change, the more innovation and creativity take hold in the environment.

The fear of moving from the secure known to a possible, but insecure, vision inspires and drives those with courage and spirit but immobilizes others. Even though they may realize the status quo doesn't work well, many are tied to it because they don't believe that the change will bring good results. They don't know enough about the change and they don't trust their leaders, so they are afraid. An environment of trust supports the kind of courage and spirit that enable creative responses to fear. The job of leaders is to build an environment in which trust is earned, fostered, and sustained.

Fear is the major obstacle to change. The fears of individuals, such as fear of failure and fear of catastrophe, prevent them from performing at their best and from acting independently. Leaders are responsible for replacing individual workplace fears with trust, but leaders have three misplaced fears of their own that halt their ability to self-confidently lead their troops through successful change efforts:

1. Fear that the change process will create more internal tension

2. Fear that the majority are opposed

3. Fear of "troublemakers"

Debilitating Fears – for Leaders
1. Fear of More Tension

"Creative tension"[2] is not the same as "emotional tension." Leaders who fear tension because they don't understand the difference and don't prepare their troops in advance to recognize and use it creatively and productively fall into a trap — an avoidable trap — that disables them and their organizations.

There is always a gap between vision and reality. Picture yourself as a trapeze artist. The trapeze you are on is safe and secure. It is scary to let go and take the leap, no matter how practiced you are or how much you want to move forward to the other side, but the desire to move on to the next one stirs your mind to design the strategy, to do the calculations to make a successful jump. That's creative tension at work — it fuels innovation. In contrast, emotional tension is debilitating.

Similarly, the gap between today's reality and tomorrow's vision creates an energy that motivates people to develop wonderful new solutions and strategies. That's creative tension, but the gap also leads to feelings of anxiety. Will it work? Will it help the company? How will it affect my job and my department?

The gap between vision and reality frequently appears to be "pie in the sky" or "grasping at straws." Dissenters use these words to discount and ridicule change initiatives. They use the change plans to illustrate their views about the incompetence of their leaders. With a leader they trust, people can get through the anxiety fairly quickly and consistently.

Instead, many organizations encountering this emotional state of anxiety lower the vision or goals. They mistakenly believe that a less-ambitious vision or smaller step will solve the problem or achieve the goal, minimize apprehension, and keep everyone happy.

Wrong.

The majority of people, who might otherwise get on board with the ambitious vision or aggressive change, become discouraged when they hear only negatives and they are not inspired by the watered-down approach. They give only lukewarm support to the effort. The watered-down approach frequently starts a downward spiral leading to mediocre success or even failure, as organizations seek "safe," consensus solutions.

Committed, strong leaders who forge ahead with the visionary plan, who communicate with and involve their people at every step, will quickly turn anxious thoughts to enthusiasm for accomplishment. Noted playwright Somerset Maugham said, "Only mediocre people are always at their best." Leaders must face the fear in themselves and their organizations and use the reality/vision gap to generate creative energy for change.

In *The Fifth Discipline*[3], Peter Senge described the human urge to move from where we are to a desirable dream of the future. The dream causes a powerful natural pull that leads individuals to seek resolution. Strong leaders understand this pull and seek ways to build and sustain this natural innovative urge in their people. Good leaders learn to involve others in planning and implementing, to communicate activities to all as much as possible, and then to MOVE!

Creative tension is the fear of moving across an abyss — from the secure known to a possible, but not yet known, vision. In bureaucratic entities — government and education in particular — people find daring to jump most difficult. The problem is that bureaucratic cultures and environments don't promote or reward individual or group risk-taking. Today, every industry is in crisis, every tradition is challenged. *Mission* is easy. *Vision* is tough. As poet Robert Frost said, "The only way out is through."

The big gap between the dream (vision) and the current situation is a source of energy. Without a gap, there would be no need for action towards the vision. The gap itself releases creative energy. Leaders who understand the importance of the creative tension dynamic and how to use it can help their organizations tap this energy to build innovative and sustainable solutions.

2. Fear that the majority is opposed

Too many leaders wait until they think they have a consensus to move forward because they fear a revolt or are afraid that they will be overwhelmingly criticized. There is almost always a misperception about the majority opinion.

Picture a bell curve. Typically, 20% of any population immediately support beneficial change. They see beyond obstacles to the benefits and quickly jump on board.

Another 60% are more cautious; the remaining 20% dislike change in general and prefer to stay where they are. Transparency and an aggressive communication effort make the difference for the majority 60%. Once stakeholders understand the change, realize the long-term benefits, understand the obstacles, and see that people they respect support the change plan, they also will support it.

When the 20% who dislike change understand that a majority of the stakeholders approves the plan and is moving to implement it, most of them will change their opinions rather than be left out. They will proactively and positively participate in planning for the change. The remaining 5% will never support the new plan and will continue working vigorously to undermine the change.

The 5% hard-core negative group is always the most vocal. I have seen many situations in which leaders were convinced that a majority was opposed to the plan because the 5% show up, write lots of letters and call. The courageous action that good leaders must take (once they assure themselves that a beneficial change is necessary) is to move quickly with the 20% vanguard while taking steps to prove that those opposed are only a small minority and to provide substantive information to the cautious 60% majority (see *Figure 3.2*).

Leaders who wait to find an approach that will make everyone happy risk minimizing and perhaps never achieving long-term success. Watering down the plan disappoints the energized, motivated 20% vanguard who helps inspire the majority. Trying for consensus enables the small, vocal minority to gain power and undermines even more the now diluted, no longer "strategic" plan or change.

Typical Dispersion of Attitudes Toward Change

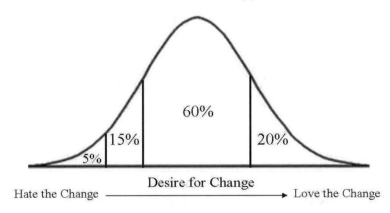

60%

15%

20%

5%

Desire for Change

Hate the Change ⟶ Love the Change

Figure 3.2

3. Fear of Troublemakers

This is the fear that identified opponents of the plan will jump out at any time and sabotage the effort. The problem with this fear is that the identified "troublemakers" are potentially a valuable asset. At a minimum, they are the voice of many other, less-outspoken critics. They typically represent an important perspective or see an issue within the proposed plan that really needs to be solved. The "troublemakers" are usually informal leaders within the troops who are not afraid to speak out and to be openly disruptive. They are people who have the self-confidence to say, "The Emperor has no clothes!"

As long as formal leaders try to keep the door to the executive decision tower closed and put chairs against it, there is always the possibility that rebel troops may break it down. If leaders open the doors, however, let the upstarts in and listen to them respectfully, the results will be positive — both in the current situation and even more so for future changes.

I have seen potentially disastrous problems averted by listening to "troublemakers" and involving them (carefully) in design teams. Once they are listened to and constructively involved, they become strong leaders for the desired change.

What's common to all three of these fears, and how do leaders build courage, rather than fear, as a management habit? They prepare well, they communicate significantly, and they MOVE FORWARD confidently.

Keys to Building Trust and Minimizing Fear

"He who hesitates is lost" is especially true in times of rapid or major change. If leaders don't move forward expeditiously, dissidents build on the fear of others to promote greater fear, which erodes support within even the most convinced of troops.

Fear is the villain in change efforts; courage is the champion trait required for success. Courage grows as Trust grows. Relevant information (vs. data) and effective communication are the biggest antidotes to fear, mistrust, and jealousy. They are the best tools to use to combat fear and to build Trust.

The *Wood County* story in *Chapter 1 — Common Knowledge* described community members who opposed progressive changes envisioned by county leaders. They used the newly introduced development strategy, a nine-town collaborative solution to the County's economic woes, to write new battle cries. The only strategy that effectively counters negative messages, builds confidence in leaders, and motivates people to positive action is to change the organization's *modus operandi* to one that strengthens trust: All activities are accomplished with open communication and involvement, good information, and obviously transparent actions.

Wood County, Part 2

The leaders of Wood County approved a three-step approach to an economic development plan:

- *Formal and informal leaders from private companies and government agencies, community, education and youth organizations, and social groups provided insights. They described the residents' attitudes and concerns. They also suggested economic development strategies for their communities.*

- *The first county-wide, professionally designed and analyzed survey, developed around the interview comments, was amazingly successful; over 70% of surveyed residents responded. Analysis of the results showed overwhelmingly positive and supportive attitudes about the change process, consistent views about the major problems facing the County, and*

. *support for new directions. Negative views about economic development represented only 8% of the population.*

- *The interview and survey results were openly and honestly communicated and discussed in open meetings throughout the community. Local media observed the process, did radio interviews, and wrote positive articles and editorials on the strategic planning purpose and process.*

The positive response and excitement that was generated in the community diminished the fears and strengthened the leaders. They moved forward aggressively with the final stage: community-wide planning. Ultimately, 300 people participated in the assessment and design of alternative solutions.

> "Confidence isn't the absence of fear; it's how you act in spite of the fear. Confidence isn't waiting until you feel totally ready to do something. If you're waiting for that feeling, you'll never do anything."
> — **Barbara de Angelis**,
> in *Women of Courage*
> by **Katherine Martin**[4]

Fear is always with us; it is a part of human nature. The challenge is: How do leaders reduce fear and support responsible risk-taking? How do leaders free potential entrepreneurs within the organization to take initiative in putting their ideas for improvement, for growth, for creative new products or services into play? The solution is to build an environment of Trust, where fear of reprisals, ridicule, or sabotage is not a factor, where good communication and information-sharing processes regularly surface and spotlight examples of individuals who took risks (large and small) and were supported in doing so.

The job of leaders is to build an environment and a culture in which Trust can be built, rebuilt, and fostered constantly. We all come into the world as babes with total trust. That trust diminishes with every life experience. Each new environment or event affects our ability to trust.

By the time we enter the work world, a new environment that absorbs most of our waking time and interactions, our Trust level is substantially less than when, as children, we were willing to try anything new, to learn anything new, to risk "NO" constantly, to dare new activities or encounters.

Experienced music teachers tell me that 4th graders are at the optimum age to learn that challenging instrument, the violin. One progressive school provides a violin class (and violins) to all 4th graders as part of the required curriculum. By then, students have developed enough to learn the violin and also still have the trust and confidence to eagerly tackle daunting challenges without fear. After 4th grade, the balance starts tipping; that courageous, confident attitude falters at a fairly rapid rate.[5]

After young adults finish their educations, each new company or position they join brings opportunities to either increase or diminish their level of Trust in their work community. Sadly, the norm is usually the latter. Employees too frequently learn to Fear rather than to Trust.

Building Trust isn't easy; there are too many impediments, even in an honest and transparent work environment. Each person's previous work environments build new and strengthen old mental models[6] that impede ready acceptance of new concepts and willingness to take risks. The challenge for leaders is to listen deeply, learn attitudes and behaviors, and develop ways to share knowledge so that employees and other key stakeholders understand. That takes time, practice, and reinforcement of messages in order to replace negative habits or attitudes with open, trusting ones.

Entities that consistently win competitive wars, overcome unforeseen disasters, and constantly innovate have environments that nurture high levels of Trust. In order to build Trust, the organization needs leaders at all levels who can develop and use effective tools to build unity — *a collective heartbeat*. These leaders know how to link and connect, to affirm and reward, to communicate information broadly and deeply, and to work selflessly to develop their people's abilities, team by team and individual by individual. Once developed, that environment can weather many storms, as great coaches like Chip Kelly, Clive Charles and Phil Knight have proven.

Fears That Cause Disengagement and Sabotage – for Employees

Jackie Babicky[7], advisor to business owners and government, developed this list of employee fears:

- Failure

- Looking foolish – "When something's changed and I didn't know about it or when everyone knows how to do something but me."

- Being "wrong" — defense mechanisms are strongly in place by age three, according to Argyris (the inventor of double-loop learning)[8]

- Not being able to "keep up" — can't adapt fast enough to changes

- Not being able to learn new things — especially the Internet, social media, new software

- Being blamed — being made the scapegoat as the one who caused the loss of money, loss of customers, or loss of organizational success

- Not fitting in — not wearing the right clothes, saying the right thing, or not knowing the culture or the customs

- Isolation, being shunned — "No one will include me in the social part of work or pass on the jokes to me or help me before I make a fool of myself."

- Not getting the information necessary to accomplish work

- Getting passed over for promotion or pay increases

- Not being treated fairly

- Losing advantage — "Others will know things and I will not so they will get some kind of beneficial advantage."

- Fear of repercussions — most particularly the ones that are not visible so "I will have no defense from them."

- Fear of Success — fear of not being able to meet new requirements for a job in personal presence, work performance, or the ability to manage others or to meet expectations

These two major fear areas (for leaders and for employees) inhibit or lead to outright sabotage of change efforts. Getting beyond these fears to gain the trust and collaboration of all stakeholders is a central concept of a resilient DNA. Consistent, powerful counter-forces are needed to replace fear-inducing environments with trust-full ones that stimulate organization-wide innovation and commitment to accomplish goals. How to achieve this transition is explained in the remaining chapters.

Powerful counter-forces start with small, basic-level changes in communication processes and in work structure (to enable sharing and involvement). Small, consistent changes always have a much greater impact on building Trust than the showy, obviously calculated major projects many leaders use in their attempts to accomplish organizational transformation.

Most people automatically distrust major change efforts based on their past experiences with highly promoted projects. New, organization-wide tools, processes, and structures can certainly yield significant beneficial results, but only when the changes (like strategic plans, process mapping, and similar approaches) are accompanied by basic environmental ones, for example, major improvements in internal communication, greater transparency, and expanded sharing across departments.

Misty Woods, Part 2

At Misty Woods, Inc., the example of inadequate communication both across the company and within departments described in Chapter 2 — Chemistry 101, *there was little Trust for other departments, despite a culture of basic respect for and honesty with one another. The solution to improving trust was to create many more opportunities for sharing across departments through more substantive meetings and more collaboration (working on problems with representatives from other departments and deeper information-sharing). These activities built greater understanding of other departments' needs, objectives, and issues and also greater awareness of impediments, problems, and individual and collective responsibilities. Finger-pointing ended and speedier, more-effective problem-solving became the norm.*

Increased understanding and involvement of others built confidence in the beleaguered finance department and led to shared responsibility for process and system improvements by all departments. The finance department manager became a trusted star player at Misty Woods, rather than a criticized and unwanted player in key projects.

Trust is built through little signals that invite participation and show an intention to listen and involve others. Many tools are available for building trust, but first, leaders must communicate their openness and desire to share information transparently.

Here are a few small ways to display openness:

Building Trust Rules

1. Always Meet on Their Turf

When trying to learn someone's perspective and gain their trust, always meet on their turf. Home turf creates a more comfortable feeling for the visited person, who feels more in control. Protective defenses drop; the person is more open to listening. You can also learn more on both a physical and intuitive level. Instead of the old mantra, "Put yourself in a power position, get them to come to you," inconvenience *yourself* and not the other person if you truly want to gain knowledge and build Trust.

The same basic concept relates to table position at in-person meetings. Unless there is a logistical problem (for example, you are leading the meeting and the only way to see everyone is by being at the head of the table), sit within the group, not at either end of the table. Sitting within the group gives you a more inclusive aura and sends the unspoken signal that you are seeking informed collaborators, not silent followers.

2. Get There Early

Get there *early* in all situations. Early arrival helps you to prepare, enables you to scope out the situation and to become comfortable with the group as it grows, and provides opportunities to observe antagonists and supporters and relate to them informally. Being early gives you a boost in building a cohort of outsiders.

Everyone knows the benefit of arriving early to meetings and events, but the benefits also hold true for situations within your organization.

3. Advance Work Shows You Care

When you are about to embark on a plan, a negotiation or a major change, you probably do advance work to learn about the people who will be involved and their environment, their culture, their concerns, their history (individually and organizationally) and needs.

Within an organization, the same Trust concept applies. On new projects, plan to encounter and to learn about people who will be involved in advance of meetings, whether electronic, telephonic, or in-person. Your effort to learn about them, which will become obvious once discussions begin, signals your desire to understand them. It shows that you care — both about them and about the project — and that you take your responsibility to assure success seriously.

The result of little steps, in building trust and in building a successful plan, is increased potential for successful achievement of your objectives.

Wood County, Part 3

The people of Wood County were so contentious and angry that others in the government community told me not to take on the county-wide Strategic Planning project. They explained that the people in the County don't like outsiders, especially not those sent by the government. Many residents of Wood County had moved there because they thought that government regulations were unreasonable and homeowner association requirements were unnecessarily restrictive in urban areas. Now, in this very rural area, they were confronting some of the same issues. They were understandably angry: government actions, spurred by good motives on issues like protection of the spotted owl species but not thoughtful of human impact, shut down the forests to logging, which led to closure of lumber mills. The result was loss of jobs in an area where there were few job opportunities outside of wood products and government.

Government actions to shut the forests to logging in an effort to protect an endangered species didn't sufficiently consider the effect on people's lives. The solution to the problem wasn't sufficiently complex; it wasn't balanced. Now, the only way to counter the problem caused by overly-aggressive government actions was to meaningfully involve the affected people in plans to develop the County's economy.

Diverse groups came together, worked hard, and created the first-ever, Wood County Strategic Plan. This was an incredible feat, given the contentious, competitive groups and towns in this depressed rural community. The County Chair had tears in his eyes as he watched hundreds of team members from the County's nine towns (many of them former combatants) celebrate the Plan's successful completion.

People who are sincerely listened to, involved in designing solutions, and spoken to with honesty and total transparency, want to help with positive changes. People want to use their skills and experiences to help make things better. It's part of human nature. They only act collaboratively, positively, when they *trust* their leaders and each other.

Because most people have a lifetime of trust-damaging events behind them, only strong evidence can change the dynamic. The evidence includes first, a catalyst from outside to signal the change. It also includes obviously transparent actions by their leaders. Most importantly, it requires *consistent* honest talk from leaders and meaningful involvement of people in the change process to keep trust going and to embed it as part of the organization's environment and culture.

The Trust Goal for leaders:

      a. **Transparency + Involvement = Growth in Trust**
      b. **Growth in Trust = Commitment to Initiatives**

PART 2 – ABILITY

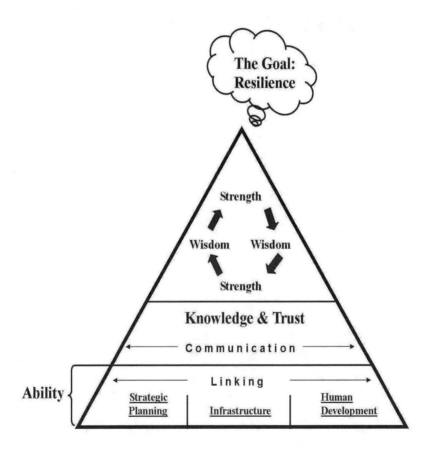

Chapter 4:
Real Involvement

Changing from "They did this to us!" to
"I helped to make this happen!"

Figure 4.1

Patemco, Part 1

The air was filled with anticipation. Twenty key leaders could barely contain their excitement. Gathered from around the country, they were together for the first time in the 25-year history of Patemco for an operations planning event. The CEO/ founder, a charismatic, gifted speaker, writer, brilliant strategist — was about to kick off a new era.

Bruce, who tightly controlled this successful communications company, realized that he must now open up his central management. Like an ant-colony queen, all organization knowledge and coordination emanated from his huge mind; but, unlike the ant colony, Bruce's lieutenants received little knowledge about the roles of other leaders except through Bruce. Bruce held all the organization knowledge and coordination under his personal command; his lieutenants' only links to each other were through him. He shared little about the overall endgame or about other divisions' activities. Rumors and suspicions about other managers' motives and activities ran rampant. This toxic situation created constant small fires and more work for the overloaded central office staff and for Bruce himself.

As demand for Patemco's products increased, the company's ability to respond effectively decreased; product and service quality suffered and competitors gained strength. Both central office staff and program managers were frequently overwhelmed by crises in their efforts to respond to new client and new program demands in a timely manner. Key managers threatened to leave.

Ownership — More Than Employee Engagement

Anxiety about the future, mistrust of other people's motives, fear that actions of others might negatively affect their own activities and future success, envy of others' promotions and successful projects: This litany of negative mental messages daily impedes active engagement and vigorous, confident progress on improvements and goals. When few opportunities exist for meaningful dialogue and interaction, especially across departments, anxieties and suspicions take hold in an organization, no matter how good the goals or the Mission. Something stronger is needed to counter negative attitudes, influences and emotions.

Meaningful involvement, promoted extensively, is the most powerful motivator and most effective way to achieve change. When stakeholders believe that change will be beneficial to the company, their department, and their jobs, they give and do their best. When employees desire and own the change, they fully commit to its success.

Three cognitive conditions are essential to build the total commitment that overcomes negative messages and prevails despite setbacks. Employees and other involved stakeholders must have:

1. *Full understanding of the change or goal on a continuous basis.* Very good communication processes (see *Chapter 2 – Chemistry 101*), are required to achieve full understanding and keep it updated.

2. *Belief that the change will benefit their job, their team, and the company.* An environment of Trust (see *Chapter 3 – The New Art of War*) enables belief.

3. *Belief that the change can and will happen.* This belief is accomplished and supported only when employees are fully informed and involved, when they *own* the change or goal.

These three conditions build on each other and reinforce each other. Together they create the *desire* to make changes and reach goals. Employees fully understand only within an environment of trust and meaningful involvement. An environment of trust exists only with the open communication that builds full understanding. True belief that the goal will happen occurs only when there is true understanding of the change and within an environment of trust.

Without the meaningful involvement that leads to whole-hearted commitment, when difficulties arise, employees typically say, "The President (or a manager, or a consultant, or the Board) came up with this. I knew it wouldn't work." The best way to combat that predictable reaction before it occurs is to consistently reinforce, in words and actions, the message: "This is *our* plan; *we* have to make it work. If you see a problem or a possible improvement, devise a solution and share it. We need your ideas. If you don't have a solution, at least share the problem, as soon as you can."

That was the message Ted received during the merger that led to Crossbow Enterprises, described in *Chapter 3 – The New Art of War.* Ted accepted the message and agreed to be a supporter rather than a detractor because the message was delivered with honest, open listening and communication. When Ted joined the team, the processes that involved and informed him constantly reaffirmed the value of his work.

Of course, good listening and sincere promises to involve people is only the first step. Delivering on the promise requires an infrastructure that will assure performance. The organization's structure, processes and systems must support *broad* input and *effective* involvement. The infrastructure must also be able to constantly reinforce the message that each person and group is not only involved but also is part of a larger team working to accomplish the changes.

Full awareness of linked activities, *working in concert across departments,* builds organizational knowledge and the ability to act with *a collective heartbeat.* Full awareness reassures stakeholders that their skills will be used and all the necessary organization resources will be employed to assure successful change. Full awareness helps everyone in the organization to understand that the change can and will happen.

Meaningful involvement is more than *kaizen*[1] or employee engagement.[2] Meaningful involvement leads to commitment at a deeper, emotional level. When a plan fails, it is frequently because naive leaders think it is sufficient for them to say, "Here is the new plan. Now, let's all join together and do it!" But requests alone, even from strong leaders, aren't enough to motivate people deeply enough to change the way they perform their jobs or to over-come their previous concerns about the company and their role in it.

One of the great employee fears, described in *Chapter 3 – The New Art of War,* is that they aren't good enough, that they won't be able to accomplish the job or that they may fail because they don't have the knowledge or skills. That personal fear is transmitted to each project or change that their organization wants to accomplish. Each employee or stakeholder, seeing the planned change from their job's perspective or from looking at just the skills of the people in the organization they know and from the perspective of their past history with the organization, may believe that the project is impossible and can't possibly succeed.

Individual workers begin to believe that planned changes will happen only when they themselves are meaningfully involved with leaders and other team members (including some from other departments), when they see the new tools and processes that will be used, and when they experience the creative results of group synergy. Their personal attitude changes to a positive one. Their fear dissipates and enthusiasm takes its place.

Ownership — *Emotional* (not just rational) Commitment: Crossbow Enterprises, Part 2

At Crossbow Enterprises, the new entity formed in the merger of three not-for-profits described in Chapter 3 – The New Art of War, *employees and members of each organization learned about teams that were being formed to plan new programs, determine future uses for all facilities, discuss governance of Crossbow, and plan for combined finances and personnel. They heard about planning activities from their friends and fellow employees who were first involved in the effort; they became curious about what would happen next. They responded to invitations to attend initial meetings of the next phase in droves.*

At the meetings, when employees and members heard more about the plan details and saw the involvement of others they trusted and respected, they volunteered to help with planning tasks. They took responsibility for getting their tasks done because they didn't want to let down their friends and co-workers. They developed new working relationships; they committed to the success of each planned step. The project moved forward — faster than scheduled in the Merger Plan — because they were enthusiastic about making Crossbow happen, despite their earlier doubts and fears.

When people thoroughly understand a problem or opportunity, personally see the benefits, help to develop the solution and create the implementation steps, they deeply commit to making it work. When the inevitable difficulties arise, they don't lose faith; they still believe in the plan. More important, when they encounter barriers or problems, people who are fully aware and involved are able to develop solutions and work around difficulties *on their own.* They thoroughly understand where the Plan came from and where it is going, why, and how. So they know, better even than outside experts, how to refresh the solution and make it even stronger.

There are two wonderful words that describe what happens when people work together:

⇒ Synergy: the working together of two or more people, organizations, or things, especially when the result is greater than the sum of their individual effects or capabilities; the correlated action of two organs or parts of the body working together, like two muscles do to create one function.[3]

⇒ Synthesis: a new unified whole resulting from the combination of different ideas, influences, or objects.[3]

Synergy occurs when two or more people work together collaboratively. The most creative genius in the world can accomplish even more when brainstorming with others. That wonderful, creative result of synergy can happen, given a fertile environment, in every team or group of individuals. It is truly amazing to see what happens when people who may never have worked together before are brought together, given good information (not data), and provided a secure forum for discussion! Ideas and strategies develop that are better than any one individual in the room could conceive. Ideas of one person trigger ideas of others; the original idea is expanded, amplified, and vitalized by others.

An additional benefit of collaborative planning is that everyone in the room, to the extent they have an opportunity to contribute and to offer opinions about pitfalls, risks and benefits, sees and understands the *context* for the strategy and development of the Plan. Because of their participation, people can apply the concept or strategy to themselves, to their work, and to their departments. They HEAR discussion of the risks and benefits and have an opportunity to offer dissent, criticism, or support. They HEAR both sides of issues, their own and the views of others; differences are blurred; synthesis occurs. Participants in the planning session can explain the strategy to others along with the pros and cons; they can promote and also defend it.

With knowledge acquired during the planning process, people are then *empowered* to represent and apply the Plan. Others, outside the planning teams, hear the news. They see that people they know and respect as leaders or peers are involved; they talk about the Plan *details* around the water cooler, at breaks or at social gatherings. When questions or problems arise, they ask these knowledgeable friends about it instead of letting their doubts or concerns fester. Problems are resolved at a very basic, peer-to-peer level, before they become bigger problems.

In contrast, when significant stakeholders or stakeholder groups are *not* included, the plan or new direction is always negatively affected. For every worthwhile plan I observed that failed to achieve its potential, inadequate communication and involvement were root problems. While *acting as one, with a collective heartbeat,* can virtually guarantee success, the lack of *meaningful* involvement of key players (both leaders and non-leaders) will always lead to plan failure, to less than full success, or to much greater than necessary expenditure of resources (both time and dollars).

So, who is a significant stakeholder? Whom do you need to involve? A significant stakeholder is any person or group who will be affected either in the implementation process or from its result. The error most organizations make is in including only *primary* players needed to effect the action or those most *directly* affected by the project result. Major problems most often begin when the changes start touching those who are indirectly or secondarily affected, both in development of the plan and as it begins to roll out. Without the earlier involvement of these related, but not primarily affected, groups, it is impossible to develop a full solution that will have substantive, sustainable results.

Barriers to Meaningful Involvement and Roads to Unity[4]

Workplace myths cause most leaders to limit the number of people who will be involved in planning for new directions. Recognizing and understanding these negative myths for what they are is the first step toward achieving meaningful involvement. The solutions are found in understanding the myths.

> "Find a job you love and you will never have to work a day in your life."
>
> — **Confucius**

Myths that Inhibit Meaningful Involvement

1. The "wrong" people (i.e., "troublemakers") will take over the teams and thwart the plan.

2. You need to wait until you perceive that the majority supports the plan before involving more than a few people or the process will get bogged down.

3. Involvement of many people will extend the process unnecessarily and will distract too much from getting regular work done.

The "unnecessary and damaging burden" myths cause leaders to avoid involvement of significant numbers of people early in the problem solving process. But, upon analyzing the myths, it becomes clear that earlier and greater involvement, handled skillfully, actually leads to huge benefits.

1. Myth that the wrong people (i.e., "troublemakers") will take over the teams and thwart the plan

The error in this myth is that most "troublemakers" are really potential assets. They shouldn't be avoided. Often, the root of their concerns is shared by others throughout the organization. "Troublemakers" are usually just more direct, more overt, and more willing to challenge their leaders. They are also more outspoken, more courageous people. You fall into a lethal trap if you ignore or avoid them; they gain more power among their peers this way. They also gain ammunition to criticize management for not wanting to listen to other opinions.

How do you disarm "troublemakers"? Pick the most articulate and rational "troublemaker" leaders. Appoint them to a change team, one that has a strong, competent leader.

If you are the leader of the team with a perceived "troublemaker," assure that the team involves and openly listens to the "troublemakers" because: a) you will learn about issues that will help you to build a better plan, and b) listening and involving "troublemakers" takes some of their ammunition — the perception that management doesn't want to listen and doesn't understand the problem, and c) frequently, as with Ted at *Crossbow*, this articulate team member becomes a very effective leader in the change effort or new direction.

2. *Myth that you need to wait until you perceive that a majority supports the plan before involving many people.*
The problem is that if you wait for that perception to change, meaningful involvement will never happen. Almost always, although they appear to be a majority, the most vocal critics represent only about 5% of the population group (see *Figure 4.2*).

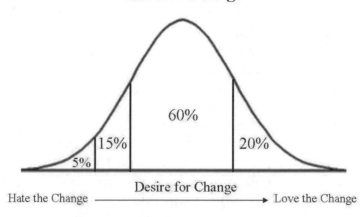

Typical Dispersion of Attitudes Toward Change

Figure 4.2

How do you disarm the vocal minority? While selecting the most articulate and rational of them to be on teams, also develop hard data about what the real majority thinks. Depending upon the situation, the culture and the depth of the problem, use focus groups, brown-bag sessions, interviews, or surveys. Or several of them, if necessary. Use expert, objecttive facilitators and specialists to assure accurate and valid results that will be credible — preferably use outsiders. Summarize the data and communicate the results loudly!

3. *Myth that involving many people will extend the process and distract from getting regular work done.*

The *Crossbow* example in *Chapter 3 – The New Art of War* demonstrates that involving people at many levels and areas saves time not only in the long run but immediately.

How does involving more people early on save time? Because of their involvement in the planning stage, people's enthusiasm and excitement grows; they willingly do more and get it done in shorter time. In the long term, you also save training and learning time. When you begin implementation, many people already understand the basics and at a much deeper level. They can immediately apply the concepts to their work. They can also help to train their co-workers and serve as resources in training sessions later. Then, as problems arise, they already know the basics to develop solutions. The time to effective application is much shorter, implementation problems are much fewer, and problem-solving is much faster and more effective.

Even when leaders understand the benefits of involvement and include representatives of many affected groups in the planning and implementation processes, the culture (or tradition) in some organizations is a barrier (especially for new leaders) to building unity through greater involvement: "That's not how we do things here," "The troops won't like it; they won't want to participate." Identifying and facing these traditions is the first step. Solutions to change the traditions and build roads to unity are found within the barriers themselves.

Barriers to Involvement
1. Differences of opinion always appear larger than they are and create unnecessarily negative environments.

2. Both "Top down" and "Bottom up" planning approaches work against meaningful involvement.

3. Company "Politics" inhibits sharing and trust needed for meaningful involvement.

As with most problems, issues and barriers, the solutions are found by analyzing the problem. It especially helps to look at the reverse side of the issue or barrier to question "why?"' In most cases, the reverse of the common approach is the better solution:

1. *Differences appear larger than they are.* Leaders hamper their ability to accomplish change by focusing on the differences of opinion or attitude, rather than on the similarities. The leaders get bogged down (and make the change much more difficult than necessary) by spending too much time on perceived differences. Most often, differences are not as significant as they first appear.

How can you avoid focusing on differences? Most groups automatically focus first on negatives and differences when they get together to discuss issues or resolve problems. Interestingly, in contrast, when *individuals* meet for the first time, they usually notice their similarities, not their differences. They ask one another where they came from, what schools they went to, about their jobs and common interests; they are alert to connections. People love to talk about what they have *in common*! It's part of human nature.

Taking a clue from this natural desire of the human species to connect with one another, groups move closer together when leaders shift their focus to listen for and find similarities first, then reinforce the common ground as they facilitate the discussion on issues. The remaining real differences in opinion diminish in size and number, the areas of disagreement become grayer.

Differences are much more easily resolved when groups realize the extent of their similar opinions. The attitude of the group changes, too; it becomes more communal. Leaders can use the areas that everyone agrees upon as "bridges" to build common solutions or compromises in areas where the perceived differences are much clearer and smaller.

2. *Neither "top down" or "bottom up" are ideal ways to plan for change.* The two most frequently used ways to plan for a change are:

   a) *Top Down:* Leaders from directly affected areas of the organization assemble to analyze the situation, develop solutions, and design implementation steps. Then they present the plan to the most affected stakeholders (frequently in large groups) for Q&A and input.

Only the bravest employees speak up. By the time most stakeholders hear about it, the plan is mostly a *fait accompli.*

The resulting problem is that only the involved management leaders feel ownership for the solution. All others may know about some specific problems but don't know if those problems were considered. They don't know enough about other related problems that influenced development of the plan or about alternatives that were discussed. They aren't sure that the solution will work and they can't run it past their cohort for their reactions, either. As a consequence, when the solution is introduced, most people give it only perfunctory support.

b) *Bottom-up:* Leaders send questionnaires out company-wide or to major affected groups in a very visible attempt to show that they are including everyone in the planning stage. They ask about attitudes, needs, perceptions, and suggested solutions.

The problem with this approach is that most people receiving the questionnaire don't have a sufficient context for answering the questions effectively, don't fully understand the history of the issue, and don't have a common starting point for their responses. They each see the issue from the vantage point of the few episodes to which they may have been exposed or from general knowledge about the issue.

When the leaders receive the responses, they see irrelevant suggestions, too general to turn into strategies or not sufficiently on point. One of two things usually happens:

1) Leaders discount much of the survey results and arrive at their own solutions. The surveyed groups feel that they weren't heard or that their answers were ignored.

2) Leaders attempt to configure a solution that includes all the different perspectives and, hopefully, achieves consensus. This approach results in broad, general, and unfocused solutions, which no one owns and many criticize as ineffective.

How do you assure that both management and staff levels, in all affected areas of the organization, are appropriately involved? The best way is a combination of top-down and bottom-up in an iterative process. For example, *Patemco*'s objective (introduced at the beginning of this chapter) was to develop a more collaborative style of management. The President wanted more sharing of knowledge and staff across divisions in order to make *Patemco* more competitive and to make better use of personnel resources during peak business times. For *Patemco*, the planning process to achieve the objective might include the following steps:

a) Key leaders, utilizing their understanding of macro trends and issues, accumulate background and history information. They develop the key goals that will address the major needs of the new direction.

b) The summarized background and history, along with a full description of the need for change and goals to achieve it, are exposed to supervisors and employees from each division who are aware of the program issues. They assess and add to the background issues and also suggest major strategies to accomplish the goals.

c) Using key themes in the program strategies, teams are formed (comprised of managers and line employees from different divisions). The groups analyze and expand the strategies and develop steps for accomplishment.

If you want effective, efficient solutions, your goal should be to inform and link your people, to the extent feasible, *before* they start addressing solutions.

3. *The political environment and history inhibit sharing and trust.* Company politics breeds fear of change and frustration in most organizations, emphasized with remarks like these:

- "You can't talk to Finance directly. You have to first go through . . . "

- "We had someone in here who tried to change the way that worked. We really needed the change but she didn't last long."

- "A group was formed to fix that two years ago. They worked hard but nothing ever happened."

In many organizations, people who try to make changes don't last long. They are criticized for "not being team players" or for "rocking the boat" even when many view their suggestions as beneficial. Seeing only frustration or their future demise, others avoid change activities. They see change projects as a potentially frustrating and non-rewarding use of their valuable time at best or as a self-destructive exercise at worst.

How to reverse this self-perpetuating negative view? A negative environment is the toughest barrier to overcome, but it can be significantly reduced by adding an outside catalyst. Because politics and tradition are embedded cultural issues, an independent, respected catalyst from outside the organization can frequently jump-start the turn-around of this self-fulfilling and destructive environment.

Unfortunately, in most organizations, the attitude is, "We have talented and smart people here. We can do this ourselves." But it is very difficult, if not impossible, to effect meaningful change with the involvement of only insiders. Major change, almost by definition, requires a catalyst from outside the organization to "open up" bureaucratic, political environments and break the cycle that perpetuates the status quo.

To effectively set the stage for the catalyst and to assure that the project is successful, highest-level leaders must agree in advance that the new direction is important enough to warrant a change in the environment. Unity starts and ends at the top.

The outside catalyst serves as a buffer to receive sensitive information from management and staff about issues and possible barriers, objectively validate and measure the issues, and summarize and camouflage the "intelligence" to protect the sources. Management can use this person, an independent and objective outsider, to facilitate establishment of new structures and processes.

This "outsider" becomes very informed but still remains unhampered by the history and "baggage" of insiders. When changes to an overly bureaucratic or tightly controlled organization are desired, this outside catalyst confirms the message leaders want to send: "It is okay to shake things up. We want that now. We invite new ways of doing things." That message energizes staff and builds their desire to do more for the organization.

Frequently, the "outsider" is automatically resented because of being an outsider. "He/she can't possibly understand this organization better than we do!" and "We don't want any change. We won't cooperate!" As displayed with *Crossbow* in *Chapter 3 – The New Art of War*, a skilled outsider will be able to assess the organization to determine the best approach to start gaining the trust of key individuals and begin the process of turning around the environment.

Plan Crashes – CEO Failure to Involve at All Levels

Change initiatives can be successfully achieved when people are involved across departments and at all levels of an organization. But the greatest barrier to success for major initiatives occurs when stakeholders at the highest level are not sufficiently involved. Abrupt and immediate plan failures occur when, for example, one of the organization's outside funders is not included in the earliest stages of planning or is not meaningfully informed throughout the planning process.

The CEO may mistakenly believe that strategic planning, organization structure, and personnel strategies are part of his or her job responsibilities and authority area and need not involve "outside" stakeholders, even key ones. Or the CEO, perceiving that certain funders or advisors are "more friendly" to his or her actions and directions than others, selects only those friendly parties to include in planning discussions.

Big mistake!

Wherever money, major direction or structure issues are concerned, critical thinkers who take their roles seriously (whether internal managers or external advisors) will be very interested and verbal.

So, those who are perceived to be outspoken critics are even more important than "friendly" parties to involve in key phases of planning. If they are not involved in the process or if they don't fully understand the plan in advance, the critical advisors or managers are likely to jump to negative opinions and develop antagonistic attitudes. Once they do, it is very difficult to move them away from their negative position.

The antidote to potential crashes caused by negative views, disparate perceptions, and a history of failed efforts is to build a people-friendly environment for change. To recap this and the previous chapters, the key to a people-friendly environment includes:

➢ Transparent processes

➢ Broad involvement

➢ Positive, logical, plan development steps, tailored to the issue (not a canned change process)

➢ Solid, well-documented background information

➢ 100% committed, enthusiastic leaders

Effective Involvement: The Road to a Collective Heartbeat

Use any new project to begin sending the message that Change toward building a more collaborative and open culture will occur. With this new project, use the simple steps outlined in *Chapter 7 — Infrastructure* and *Chapter 8 — People Focus* to establish a visible process and structure for assessment, planning, and successful implementation. This beta-test project will demonstrate for all that the organization is moving towards *acting as one*.

Patemco, Part 2

For Patemco, the tightly controlled organization described at the beginning of this chapter, the only effective solution to its growth and quality barrier was for Bruce to give up some control of Patemco's operations and to share broader organization knowledge with the previously isolated key managers. Bruce had recently learned that more information, stronger communication links, and real involvement were the keys to enable growth and improve the work environment. With changes in these areas, Patemco could accomplish more without increasing headcount.

Bruce sent a strong message when he invited his twenty most-senior people to the first organization-wide planning meeting. At the same time, Bruce also began to share his knowledge and to delegate his responsibility and authority. The unspoken message was that Bruce was opening up the organization, restructuring it, and increasing communication to a level light years ahead of the way they had worked together before. The managers were invigorated.

At the meeting, Bruce reinforced the message of positive change. From his introduction and from the level of information he imparted about the company's current status, key issues, and future plans in every division, the leaders realized that the new order was transparency and collaboration. During break-out sessions, they discussed how they could help to ease one another's workloads during their differing peak-activity times, collaborate to solve problems, and work to improve service and product quality together. Central office personnel were energized by the prospect of greater access to resources in field offices and in their new responsibility to facilitate cross-department collaboration.

Bruce took the scary step of opening the doors to his control tower. At the first planning meeting, he proclaimed a new era of shared information, responsibility, and authority and of greater individual ownership of the company's future. The result was increased capacity, greater productivity, improved product quality, and stronger commitment by all to Patemco.

Making meaningful involvement a basic value is the key to a sustainable organization that can effectively and immediately react to any assault, like the "no huddle" offense of the University of Portland lady Pilots soccer team and the University of Oregon Ducks football team. Meaningful involvement leads to the ability to act with a collective heartbeat, to organization unity and resilience.

Meaningful involvement constantly enhances all three attributes that need to be strengthened in order to motivate people to embrace change and commit to its success. Strong levels of Trust, Knowledge, and Communication drive the *desire* to do whatever is necessary to achieve success (see *Figure 4.3*). *Desire* motivates. *Ability* reinforces and supports *Desire*.

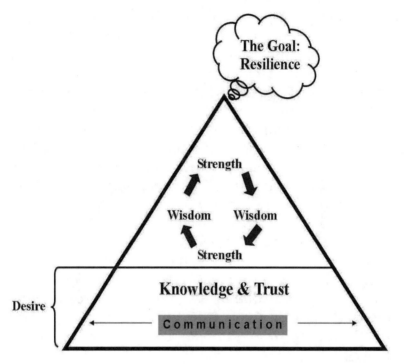

Figure 4.3

Chapter 5:
Process Power

Enabling Action through Visible,
Established Protocols

Figure 5.1

Small Business Advocate Program

I was the first Small Business Advocate for the State of Oregon, part of the Department of Economic Development, for eighteen months. During the assessment phase, we completed the first comprehensive survey of small business in the state. I also interviewed and advised over 200 small businesses in thirty-six rural and urban communities.

The consistent message I heard from the small businesses was, "Don't give us any more expensive, fancy programs. There are enough already. If you really want to help us, make it less time-consuming for us to deal with government requirements and to access existing programs. Overlapping, burdensome and inefficient processes — even the funding and resource programs established to help us — are frustrating. They cost valuable management and staff time and money in long, repetitive, duplicative documentation processes. When we have questions, we are transferred from one agency to another, which wastes more time and money. If you can improve and simplify the programs and the compliance requirements, you will save us both money and time. That's the best thing you can do for us."

Most large organizations have duplicative, out-of-sync processes, redundant forms, and conflicting information because people don't consider existing processes when building new ones. Thinking about process builds employee ownership, efficiency and effectiveness. Process thinking is inseparable from successful, sustainable change.

Bureaucratic entities give process-thinking a bad name; employees drown in unnecessary and overdone procedures. As a result, people don't consider the impact on process when developing new initiatives; they simply add more unnecessary steps and duplication.

Without effective, well-understood, and widely known processes, several problems result:

- Members of the organization don't know how to make their ideas for improvement known.

- Personnel have no confidence that their suggestions, no matter how worthy, will ever receive considered attention and evaluation.

- New programs are developed without considering already existing processes. This causes confusion, significant duplication, disconnected information and frequent error.

Employees don't trust "the system" when they don't understand how it works or don't see it work predictably and reasonably. Employees believe that company politics, rather than thoughtful consideration, determines the strategy. Each individual must understand the big-picture plan, what his/her part in it is, where and how his/her role links to others, and what the role of others is. Effective processes minimize duplication, improve customer service, and maximize the potential for dynamic improvement and future growth. Good processes enable changes to be made more efficiently and achieve more successful and more sustainable results.

Process Thinking vs. Reactionary Thinking
Process thinking versus immediate action/reaction (e.g., "Just Do It") builds ownership and much more efficient and effective solutions. Process thinking as a basic value is inseparable from achieving consistent, successful change.

Spontaneous, impatient people have a hard time with process-thinking. Today's rapid-fire computer and video games breed the opposite kind of thinking, which is detrimental to building unified, sustainable organizations. In every situation I have seen, process-thinking and -acting leads to much better solutions, more consistent success, and much greater opportunities for involvement and input at all levels of the organization.

Lack of an internal organizational *process for accomplishing change* stops progress and creativity. That may seem counter-intuitive to many people who believe that taking the time to develop ideas through a defined process stifles creativity and true change. That is true with bureaucratic, inefficient, and duplicative processes, but when there isn't a defined, rational, and visible process for making decisions, people are timid about speaking up. As a result, they feel frustrated and powerless. If they don't know there is a clear process for making their thoughts, ideas and issues known, they will believe that it's all about who can talk the loudest, who has the greatest clout and the best words, and who plays politics the best. PROCESS IS EMPOWERING to people, even if they don't understand the concept.

Where good processes don't exist, especially in mature organizations that have grown without them, it takes a major effort to put them in place. It is much simpler to begin new organizations with solid processes and grow the processes along with the organization.

Amazingly, planning processes are those least frequently in place, even in mature organizations. That is remarkable because planning processes are the most important to assure the future success, stability, and growth of the organization.

The CEO of a large international CPA firm once told me, "Don't worry about telling people *why* we need to change. Change is easy in big companies. I just say, 'Change this' and it happens. Our established structure and processes make sure it does." That may be true in the short term. But problems always arise that take too long to resolve or shake people's faith in their leaders and in the efficacy of the change. As a result, the change doesn't work and isn't sustainable. Long-term damage occurs.

Good process leads to better results for any project or change. Recently, there were allegations of voter fraud in Oregon's pioneering vote-by-mail system. Doug Lewis, the executive director of the National Association of Election Officials, commented that fraud is possible in any voting system, whether by mail or in person. He said, "If you set up your procedures correctly . . . it's more difficult than people think to mal-appropriate votes. It's your procedures that save you or do you in."[1]

Process Rule #1: Don't Rush to Implement Obvious Solutions

On the way to solving problems with good process steps, you end up solving many others that may not yet have become disruptive or glaring. You find many root causes.

That's why good process is much more effective than just implementing the solution that everyone thinks is the answer. Just implementing what appears as the obvious solution will probably never get you to the root causes.

Usually, the problem you set out to fix was just a symptom of a much bigger one. That invisible root cause will continue to aggravate the situation and unnecessarily damage the organization's potential for success. Always use a well-thought-out process to assess, develop, and implement solutions.

Good Process Helps Customers, the Bottom Line and Employee Morale: Small Business Advocate, Part 2

In response to the very clear, consistent message we heard from small businesses, the Small Business Advocate Program[1] took several steps:

To graphically display the problem for legislators and agency directors, we flowcharted the government agencies with whom two typical, successful small businesses interacted: a landscaping company and a local restaurant. The landscaping company interacted with 63 government agencies, the local restaurant with 48!

Next, 26 government agencies, from Agriculture to the State Fire Marshall, agreed to work with us to improve small business access and to reduce overlapping forms and processes. A key manager from each agency was assigned to work with the Small Business Program. Information sessions enabled the managers to learn more about each other's agencies: the extent of their programs, the type of issues they handled, and the resources they used.

Subsequent brainstorming sessions addressed major small business headaches like the hand-offs from one agency to another and from one department to another within each agency. They talked about how to improve telephone responses and do better triage to find the best place within their agency to answer callers' questions or link them with a specific person at another agency, instead of simply saying, "We don't handle that. Try calling the Energy Department." They reviewed basic forms within each agency to develop common forms that might be used by several agencies rather than requiring individual forms for similar issues.

We developed a new, computerized information database to back up a new Hot Line for businesses dealing with government compliance or trying to access government resources. Real people used the data base to triage small business problems, rather than sending the businesses off on a wild goose chase from agency to agency in pursuit of solutions.[2]

The agency managers enthusiastically began working together outside of the formal meetings to resolve some duplications and repetitious steps on their own. Their response was, "We knew that there were better ways to respond to businesses and to handle these functions across agencies, but we didn't have a forum for working on them. We wanted to improve but we didn't know where to start or how to get it done. This collaboration, new processes, and the new tools — the database and Hot Line — make work more efficient for our agencies, in addition to making it easier for businesses to access services and to comply with requirements."

In other words, the frustration and the desire to improve the ways they worked with their customer businesses existed within the agencies, but individual departments didn't have either a structure or a process for doing anything about it.

The processes for linking, communicating, and sharing developed for the Small Business project EMPOWERED the managers to work on their own department processes. Managers designed solutions after learning more about one another's structure, processes and systems. This knowledge, along with the collaborative processes and communication tools started through the Small Business project, helped to create happier, more motivated, more customer-focused managers (and employees) while enabling them to do more with the time they had available. This process and the changes managers developed resulted in greater efficiencies and a better work environment for them and their employees.

The failure to consider existing structure and process and to integrate them with those of new or revised programs causes non-integrated, duplicative processes that create missteps, redundant forms, and conflicting information. That failure unnecessarily adds to employee burdens, customer confusion and frustration, and increased costs.

Process Rule #2: Don't "Just Do It!"

For an organization that doesn't have good processes in place, it's hard to understand the value of process thinking and documented tools. It's hard to display the value of planning, as opposed to "Just do it!" That's a great mantra, but only *after* a well-thought-out plan is in place, developed by relevant and appropriate stakeholders.

Phil Knight, the Founder and Chairman of Nike and a former Price Waterhouse CPA, knew the value of good planning and processes. Most of his founding core team were CPAs and attorneys, who are schooled in and know the value of process and advance preparation.

The term "Just Do It" has, I believe, been misused and misquoted. I think it means, "Don't worry about all the potential problems, don't be afraid. You can get stuck worrying and never move forward. Once you have a good plan and good steps to accomplish it, then 'Just do it!'"

Create Faster Break-Throughs: Acrobat Instruments, Part 2

The importance of a plan and processes was really obvious with Acrobat Instruments, which, at twelve years old, was probably the biggest tiny company of my career. Ron Arculeta, the President, said, "We need to hire a PR firm to make us well-known on a national level." He said this repeatedly, but Acrobat wasn't ready yet. The policies, structure and job descriptions, and organizational processes were in the midst of implementation to prevent the constant crises that previously distracted managers and inhibited forward movement. These problems were caused by lack of policies, standard procedures, adequate documentation, etc. Decisions were made spontaneously. My response to Ron's repeated comment was, "What will you tell the PR firm? What are you going to give them? They need direction and information. You don't have that. You aren't ready."

The PR firm was hired, six months later, after a search process that included a strategic marketing plan and after basic documents were prepared to describe the company. Ron heard the finalist firms say, "Give us your company history and goals, tell us what work you have done and where it is located, describe your competitors, tell us who your current and ideal potential customers are, describe them, tell us what marketing you have done in the past and give us examples; explain where you want to go."

Acrobat now had a basic Strategic Marketing Plan available, developed by key stakeholders and advisors, and detailed backup documents prepared by staff from the Plan. When new web designers asked the same questions, the needed materials were ready.

When Acrobat later responded to a Request for Qualifications (RFQ), the Plan was used again and resulted in the largest contract Acrobat had ever signed — a national, very visible and potentially multi-project contract. The customer affirmed that they would not have awarded the project to Acrobat without the strong infrastructure: the Vision and Plan to achieve it, policies and procedures, established responsibilities, integrated systems, and personnel coaching and development.

109

All subsequent projects were developed more efficiently and more effectively and were more consistently focused on the integrated strategic marketing plan. The Vision moved forward rapidly as a result of using process *to develop the Plan and organizational materials, to design standard templates for customers and vendors, and to establish plans for human and organizational development.*

Human beings are composed of mind, body and soul. Consistent winners are created by developing all three. Organizations, made up of human beings linked through their jobs, are similarly composed of a collective mind, body, and soul. All three must be developed into high-performing components in order to enable consistent, sustainable, winning entities.

Chapter 3 — The New Art of War and *Chapter 4 — Real Involvement* describe what it takes to build the *mind* of a consistently winning organization, what it takes to enable and maintain *Desire*. Developing the *body* of a winning organization means developing *Ability* — the tangible components that, when well-formed, enable success. These tangible components support organizational Knowledge and secure an environment of Trust (see *Figure 5.2*).

The Vision and Mission, along with linked goals, strategies, and action steps, are documented in the *strategic plan*. It is the skeleton, the framework that supports the other physical components of the organization. Think of the organization structure, systems, and processes — the *infrastructure* — as well-developed muscles that connect and enable effective movement. Think of *human development* resources as the key organs of this organizational body — the heart and the lungs. They must build strength in themselves through exercise and good nutrition to propel the whole body to success and assure consistent good performance.

Process thinking is the *linking* mechanism that connects all parts of the organizational body to one another — to constantly strengthen *Ability.*

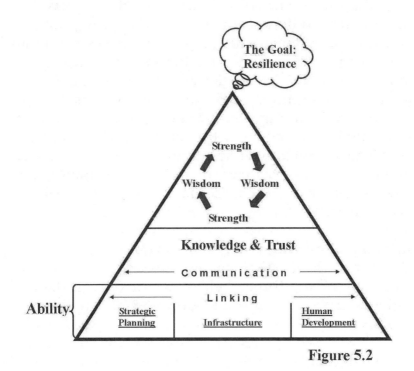

Figure 5.2

Transitioning to a team-focused, unified entity requires more than good organization structure, systems, and processes. It takes an acquired sensitivity to listen and learn from others — peer to peer and manager to staff.

Working together in teams, on projects that impact individuals and the organization, is the best way to link far-flung people (like the managers in disparate government agencies) to build the sense of unity and to ensure effective management by independent-thinking, creative people. Working in

111

teams is also the best way to achieve a collaborative environment that maximizes efficient use of human and financial resources.

Process thinking is the essential "conductive gel" of effective teamwork for accomplishing any project. It is the key element for teams to achieve effective results, the difference between just group brain-storming and successful projects.[3] Process thinking is the key to effective organizational tools, especially major ones like strategic planning, sound infra-structure, and human development programs.

Process thinking is a practiced skill that can be developed fairly quickly, but learning the concepts isn't enough to gain understanding of how it works. People have to participate in the development or change project, within teams, to gain the skill of process thinking.

Advance Planning vs. Quick Action

There are three steps to an effective, sustainable solution. In all three steps, use of a team-based process trumps immediate decision and action by leaders.

1. Determine the cause of the problem or assess need for the change.

2. Develop the solution/plan.

3. Oversee accomplishment to assure effective implementation consistent with the plan.

Good planning is an iterative process (discussed on page 93 of *Chapter 4 — Real Involvement*). Teams are a key component in all three steps, but the role of leaders differs at each step. The assess-ment step starts with the leaders, those who are the most global thinkers, whether the goal is to establish a new division, respond to a customer service problem, or boost a department's productivity. The people with the broadest perspective of the issue, one step *above* the level of the needed change, should start the assessment.

For example, if the problem appears to be within one division, the first level of planning should include the division leader, leaders of a few related divisions or administrative departments, and also one or two carefully selected officers. The officers are there not to dominate or control but to add an objective perspective to issue discussions. This group can arrive at the big-picture view of the goal or problem most effectively and efficiently.

Next, the planning dialogue should expand to include those who will lead the front lines during implementation. These supervisor-level people must learn the big-picture issues so they can later transmit this information to their troops. The expanded group provides depth in defining the problem, refining the issues, and developing the strategies. Finally, teams, including line workers, build action plans that respond to real workplace and customer situations.

Even the best leaders can't assure successful results with good leadership alone. There are too many big issues: major customers and suppliers, industry trends, external economic and financial trends, market trends, product quality and innovations, equipment and facility adequacy, production capacity, adequate inventory levels, government regulations and industry standards, outside stakeholders, to name some of them. Peripheral issues affect the success of any change effort. People who work within the change area on a day-to-day basis don't see the impact of these related issues on the problem or proposed change. It takes a combination of perspectives, at various levels and areas of the organization, to see implications and resources needed for successful results.

Good initiatives are frequently doomed due to failure to consider these broader-context factors. Failure to communicate peripheral factors and to describe the decision process *in advance* causes needless discontent and grumbling when leaders overrule the solutions that problem-solving teams developed in good faith, believing they knew all the relevant factors. A transparent decision-making process and early involvement of others outside the prime area raises awareness of implications and resources and helps assure that the solution and implementation steps include consideration of more than just the direct, immediate issues.

The countervailing problem is that the front-end planning causes impatience and misperceptions by line troops and outside stakeholders. They perceive only needless delay in solving critical problems. Communication of the planning process and its benefits helps, but doesn't totally diminish, the impatience of those outside the planning process. The trick is to balance planning with actions, high-level with operating-level involvement, throughout the planning process. As quickly as possible, begin with priority steps and the "low-hanging fruit" that come out of the initial planning stage, the most obvious solutions and the easiest to outline major steps: *Implement* and *involve*.

Implement solutions that develop from the first planning steps to give "quick wins" as planning on more complex aspects of the goal continues. Assign implementation of immediate steps to new groups, as appropriate, comprised of individuals from both within and outside the initial planning group.

Taking quick actions on the "low-hanging fruit" before planning is complete will accomplish several objectives:

1. Gets something done quickly

2. Is an exercise and a "test" of the implementation and reporting process

3. Creates a "success" that can be a visible proof of progress and the benefits of the planning process, both to the involved team and the rest of the organization, and

4. Once it is successfully implemented, provides material for building the extensive communication process that is critical for linking everyone. It helps prepare everyone for their involvement and belief in the change, to work on larger strategies and the overall goal.

Process Rule #3 – Act and Communicate Early and Often

1. Many organizations believe it is better to wait until the plan is complete to expose pieces of it, but the earliest pieces — first, the vision and the goals, then the major strategies — can be exciting and help to build momentum while everyone waits. Release the big-picture goal and framework as soon as possible, before it is fully complete and documented! Leaders are frequently afraid the early pieces may create fears and concerns, but the alternative — a void when there are recognized problems — is worse.

> 2. Document the plan process for teams, including the approval process, well in advance. Failure to communicate a clear roadmap will cause confusion and frustration as teams produce incomplete and insufficiently researched solutions that are inadequate for effective decision-making by teams and leaders.

Barrier to Good Process — The Leaders: Small Business Advocate, Part 3

The Agency Collaboration project was successful, the most successful of all the good programs developed during my stint as Oregon's first Small Business Advocate. The project required no funding and it improved efficient use of people resources. Agency personnel had more time available to work on other projects. Managers from 26 different agencies were highly motivated by one another to work on more individual agency process improvements that would help business "customers." The time spent in making those improvements was made up, many times over, by time saved in duplicative, unnecessary tasks — plus, the customers were happier.

Sadly, after I completed my 18-month loaned executive Small Business Advocate commitment, the Agency Collaboration project ended. Managers were disappointed; they wanted to do more changes but were stopped. They complained to me and to others but to no avail; there was no impetus or facilitator to continue the inter-agency process discussions. Their bosses, the Agency Directors, were fearful of the discussions and ensuing changes. Since the activities were cross-agency, there was no one Director to champion the collaboration. The Governor, the most passionate advocate for the project, was distracted by personal problems and unavailable to promote continued implementation.

Agency directors didn't want change, especially if it might mean giving up some control of their territory, even in the name of greater efficiency, productivity and customer service. Process thinking requires opening up and exposing the way things are done, which exposes duplications. Process thinking also illuminates gaps in programs and procedures, which may also be seen as failures of leadership. Both the spotlighted duplications and gaps may mean shifting or sharing of territory. That's scary for leaders, especially in governmental and other highly-bureaucratic industries.

The major message is that *process thinking* — planning, asking the right questions, obtaining good information, interacting with the right people across the organization, documenting and analyzing the collected facts — is critical to accomplishing successful change. Good process assures that each individual in the organization understands the plan, what part in the plan is theirs, where their role links to others in the organization, and what the role of others is. Good process minimizes duplication and maximizes the potential for collaboration and synergy, both immediately and with larger changes to come. The result is faster, more successful, more sustainable changes.

Grunstad Metal

Christine Gemetti didn't use good process thinking when she was hired as the first Operations Manager at Grunstad Metal, a rapidly growing manufacturing company. They had a long list of projects to accomplish and critically needed processes to design and document before numerous major contracts in process hit production at the same time. It was a perfect time to implement good process thinking.

Christine saw the long list of purchases to make and projects to be completed. She didn't carefully choose people from across the organization to plan the objectives and critical steps. She didn't determine information needed and required resources (such as people, money, facilities, equipment, and tools). Instead, she and two trusted "lieutenants" immediately began writing policies and processes, calling on target customers, making large purchases from standard vendors, and designing marketing events. Important questions went unanswered, like: "What critical information and resources are needed to plan and execute this major growth phase? What will customers, employees, or the media want to know about these activities? What will our funders ask about this plan? How will we explain it to them? What documents will we give them?"

Christine and her lieutenants simply used their individual knowledge and past personal experience to take immediate action.

The result for Christine was negative responses from customers and major stakeholders who saw and experienced major flaws in the processes and the plan. There were many costly mistakes; crises erupted in many directions. In retrospect, Christine realized the value of planning, process, involvement of others, and of documented facts and examples to coach and prepare employees — all part of process thinking.

Christine came very close to being terminated after only three months on the job. Now, before starting a project, Christine meets in groups comprised of managers and supervisors (selected from across the organization) and inside and outside specialists. Together, they complete the first level — i.e., strategic — planning. They ask each other questions, gather information, develop approaches, then involve more people, ask more questions, develop the next steps and move forward — faster and more effectively and successfully than before.

Process thinking, far from slowing progress, facilitates fast and effective accomplishment of goals. Strategic planning jumpstarts progress on any goal by underscoring and strengthening linkages. It also opens the door to quick wins in achieving goals by ensuring common knowledge *across* departments or divisions and facilitating *horizontal* linking of processes.

Acrobat Instruments, Part 3
Acrobat Instruments, eight years later with Ron Arculeta still at its helm, continues to succeed, now at a rapid growth rate, despite mega-crises and challenges. Acrobat succeeds because it built a solid strategic plan, developed strong policies and procedures, worked to develop its people and linked all through a stable process-thinking environment.

Chapter 6:
Strategic Vision
Driving Dynamic Growth and Transitions

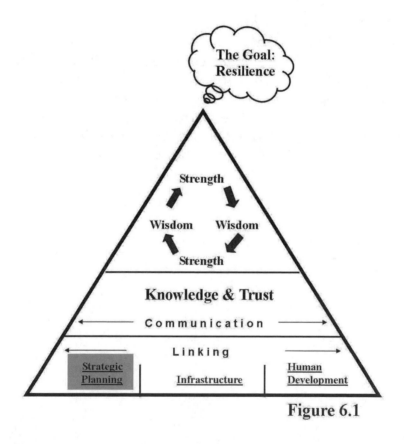

Figure 6.1

*T*ed Turner, the incredibly successful serial entrepreneur whose golden touch transforms difficult acquisitions into hugely successful endeavors, was asked about how he does it. He quoted his father's advice: "Always have a goal far greater than you think you could accomplish."[1]

Most organizations, especially their CEOs, are terrified of lofty visions. They are afraid they might not be able to reach an inspiring goal. They fear they will be criticized by stakeholders, especially funders. Worse, they may be fired for not achieving goals. But lofty visions have the power to inspire and unify teams to overcome barriers and challenges. Lofty visions also attract funders and major contributors; they amplify commitment.

It takes a courageous, self-confident leader to articulate and lead stakeholders to action on a lofty goal and vision. Examples of powerful visions that motivated companies to great accomplishment are plentiful. Fed Ex visioned: "They will get it the next day." It seemed impossible when they first exposed that Vision. But they did it. The soccer coach from tiny University of Portland told the team and the University, "We will be the best women's soccer team in the U.S."[2] That seemed like an impossible dream when he said it. People laughed. But the team did it. Mediocre, stair-step visions and goals don't inspire people to take risks and to go the extra mile to overcome tough problems and aggressively move in new directions. Lofty visions do.

Everyone loves underdogs — they fight harder and frequently win. Why do they fight harder and win against odds? Because a lofty Vision is so far out there, so compelling that it creates tremendous momentum and dynamic pressure. Individuals or groups with such visions are often unstoppable.

The little-known and little-respected University of Oregon Ducks football team came out of nowhere in 2009 with a new coach, a guy who had never been a head coach before. In his first four years as head coach at the University of Oregon, he took the team to four straight national championship play-offs. No other coach has ever done that. He inspired the team to win, a team that once went 26 seasons in a row without a bowl appearance.[3] Chip Kelly did it by changing the culture with an inspiring Vision that expected success and by equally great attention to detailed preparation.

I personally experienced the results of a lofty Vision. My first accounting-firm boss asked what my goals were. I told him I wanted to be the first woman Chair of the American Institute of CPAs. He laughed. "Don't you think you need to become a CPA first?" I almost achieved the big Vision but took myself out of the running. In the year that everyone said I was a shoo-in to be selected for that Chair position, the firm I founded merged with a national giant, KPMG Peat Marwick. Because of my new position and my new firm's policies, I was ineligible, but my Vision took me to the brink.

Clear, inspirational Vision works, even on small-scale projects.

Mercurial Academy, Part 1

Mercurial Academy, a nationally renowned school and research facility for talented and gifted students, was preparing for its annual fundraiser event and funding drive, targeted to produce over 30% of their annual revenues.

The challenge? The Great Recession was pummeling the not-for-profit industry. A scandal involving the President was all over the media. Internally, there was major personnel turnover, including the event manager. Jo Ross, the new event manager, was also aware of the organization's culture and modus operandi: *inadequate planning at a strategic level, too little cross-department communication and sharing, inadequate information systems, and a distaste for making changes. But Jo Ross believed in the strength of Mercurial's Mission and Vision, the untapped talents of its personnel, and the potential for success.*

Ignoring recommendations to drop the event's revenue goal, Jo instead increased the goal amount over the pre-Recession record success. She worked with teams to develop a new strategy for the event based on the Vision of great success. She changed the department's processes and environment to build trust and collaboration.

The result? They beat the previous pre-Recession record, in a year of horrible crisis. A department team member noted, "Everyone wonders how we achieved such great success, against such odds. I know how — we became One!"

It was the Vision. Even though a lofty vision or goal might not quite make it, it will always enable the organization to achieve much more than if they set a "safe" goal.

Strategic Vision — the Unifying Force

A dynamic, unifying Vision is the primary force that enables organizations to be the most successful they can be — at virtually anything and everything. In *Chapter 5 — Process Power*, we discussed the critical importance of horizontal integration, across departments and across divisions, to accomplish great improvements in productivity and customer service while implementing any change. To assure true innovation, however, organization-wide critical thinking, and quick response, vertical integration is even more important. Unfortunately, not many organizations take steps to build vertical integration as a basic value.

As described in *Chapter 2 – Common Knowledge*, supervisors and mid-level managers are critical in building vertical integration (see *Figure 6.2*). They are the funnel through which the Vision, developed by big-picture-thinking leaders, is passed to the troops. They are the Interpreters.

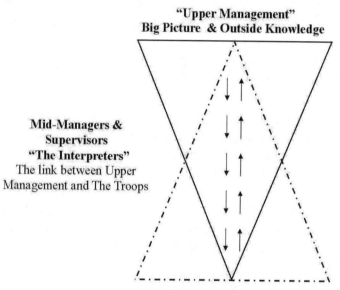

"Upper Management"
Big Picture & Outside Knowledge

Mid-Managers &
Supervisors
"The Interpreters"
The link between Upper
Management and The Troops

Detailed Information - Functions, Processes & Products
"The Troops"

Figure 6.2

Involvement of these mid-level leaders, as broadly selected as possible, is important at the second level of strategic plan development — as soon as possible after the Internal and External Assessments, after development of the future Vision and major Goals.

Chapter 5 — Process Power discussed the value of *Acrobat Instruments'* Strategic Marketing Plan.

Acrobat Instruments, Part 4

Acrobat had an incredible product and reputation within a small sphere but wasn't making much money. The first step to a solution was to understand the problem and to learn where the Company wanted to go — the Vision. The stakeholders needed a common understanding of Acrobat's Vision and opportunities, strengths and weaknesses before they could develop effective solutions. Once everyone understood and agreed on opportunities, the major stakeholders could critique and resolve the biggest impediments to achieving them.

Typically, leaders think that they know what the problem is. Acrobat's Board Chair and major funder thought he knew — the owner/CEO, Ron Arculeta, was involved in too many interesting opportunities in too many different directions that took his focus away from the core product. Crises that erupted from some of Ron's opportunities caused constant tempests that further distracted him and everyone else from using his great talent for product development and production, from marketing strategies, and from other important growth initiatives.

In Acrobat's case, as with most stalled growth and low-profitability situations, it became obvious that the company was not clear in communicating the direction and that key stakeholders didn't agree on strategies. There were multiple views on direction, resources and core problems. Given that situation, funders, key supporters, managers and troops **could not** *work together to accomplish company goals. They were all hearing different messages.*

Once Acrobat completed the important Vision development process, movement towards goals was

125

swift and effective. Strategies were developed and implemented for many different areas, all linked to achieving the unifying, lofty Vision.

Mission Is Easy; Vision Is Tough

It is important to differentiate between Vision — the pivotal piece of the Strategic Plan — and the entity's Mission — the purpose for which it was founded and continues to exist.[4] The Mission is rarely changed, usually only when the market need for the primary product or service wanes.

In contrast, Vision is the core, the heart, of the Strategic Plan or for any change or new direction. Vision alters when the organization revises the Strategic Plan. Vision *drives* the new direction to fulfillment and serves as a guide to help assure successful *change.* Giving the Vision short shrift in planning for the future, for a new direction, or for any major change, severely undermines successful achievement.

Vision is the most important but most often confused and undervalued component of the planning process. Not just because of fear of possibly not achieving the goal but also because visioning is the least tangible component and demands the most usage of right-brain functions. Visioning isn't as analytical or logical a procedure as other process components. It doesn't use typical business skills. For most facilitators, Visioning is the most difficult exercise to lead. The vital Visioning exercise relies heavily on preparation of the group mind and on synergy, a nebulous force. Although synergy can't be controlled, it can be facilitated.

Developing a truly commanding and dynamic Vision is potentially the most energizing and therefore rewarding component of Strategic Planning. It is exciting!

Frequently, organizations quickly arrive at a "Vision" upon which everyone can agree, a consensus description that actually describes the current good things the organization does rather than an image of the future. Generally, that approach results in a Vision statement that is much more of a Mission/Purpose than a Vision that describes what the organization *will be.*

Unless there is a true Vision, groups flounder in designing major strategies and become mired in debates about which roads to take because they lack the "guiding star" — the Vision. They need to collectively see and understand the future — where they are going in their journey — to effectively plan and successfully drive there.

I have observed many organizations, both civic and private, that rush to develop strategies. The leaders don't want to "waste their time" on a visioning process. To speed up the process and move on to strategies, they quickly write a broad, general statement composed of platitudes. It describes a successful current condition that could be used by many similar organizations in their industry.

This approach is especially true of governmental and large not-for-profits that want to please their publics by involving large groups of stakeholders in their planning process. The leaders usually have predetermined the major new directions and goals. Because of that, they certainly don't want to involve the large groups in an assessment process or in developing a big-picture vision that might conflict with their privately determined direction.

Typically, stakeholders each have different perspectives about the future of an organization and consciously or unconsciously work towards their own view of what it will be or how it will function. It is impossible to move forward effectively with these unspoken, unresolved disparate views of the future, let alone determine how to get there. The result is usually an unfocused mix of strategies for moving forward rather than a targeted plan for achieving an inspiring, motivating, collectively developed Vision.

When a well-defined Vision of a changed future exists, paths towards solving problems that impede growth become easier to see, design, and follow. A unifying Vision enables effective redevelopment of an entity — its structure, systems and processes — to facilitate accomplishment of the Vision. A clear and motivating Vision feeds *whole team* effectiveness, both horizontally and vertically, across the organization.

A clear vision or goal is an important part of any change project, but for an entity's Strategic Plan, a true Vision is the key to efficient, successful accomplishment versus plodding, problematic progress. Vision enables effective (linked) communication of every department's progress, thereby building unity toward accomplishment of all goals.

Visioning is a circular, iterative action. Strong processes, effective communication tools, and real understanding of the linked roles of others ensure Vision accomplishment. Similarly, a dynamic Vision enables effective improvement of all organizational components. *Chapter 7 — Infrastructure* discusses this iterative process in more detail.

Vision – A Right-Brain Exercise

A good Vision makes all decisions easier. It unifies and enables agreement on decisions much faster. So, how do you get to a real, *future-focused* Vision?

1. Don't *start* with a large group. Large group planning (more than about 10 people) complicates the initial, most strategic part of the

process. Some synergy can still occur within large groups by using break-out sessions, but the process for hearing and utilizing creative but softer voices is difficult. See *Chapter 7 — Infrastructure* for more on this concept.

2. Select the Visioning group carefully to provide different perspectives and build an environment for good synergy. Members should have diverse views and be proven, collaborative, team players who are open to new ideas. They should also have strong credentials in their areas of expertise so they will be accepted and respected by stakeholders as appropriate members of this important team.

3. Provide for good atmosphere. Environment either feeds or detracts from the group's ability to collectively create. Select a location that promotes inspiration. Create a warm, serene and joyful ambiance. An open, expansive view stimulates innovative thinking versus a room with no windows.

4. Prepare the group to brainstorm. Send the introductory, historical summaries, and basic trend information in user-friendly, quick-to-digest formats. The materials, if effectively prepared, will begin to enable the disparate views to see things from the same perspective and focus in the same directions, without getting mired in detail that might distract them from the bigger picture and their own important views.

5. Design the Visioning process to include steps that stimulate and accumulate the collective

intelligence, develop common views about the organization and its environment, and point to the desired *question* (not answer!).

6. Begin discussion with an assessment of the critical factors that affect the organization (global, national, and industry trends; status of competitors), and also an assessment of the internal situation (strengths, weaknesses, opportunities, threats) to prepare the group for Visioning. Collective knowledge-sharing helps trigger individual creativity and group unity; it stimulates synergy.

7. Select a facilitator who is highly skilled at:

   a. listening at a level where words are not yet fully verbalized and are only hinted at, frequently in a nonverbal, body-language way

   b. pulling possibilities out of individuals that they may not consciously realize are within them

   c. creating a safe and welcoming forum for individuals to freely share their words

   d. helping individuals to frame their words so that the group can hear, digest, and amplify those thoughts

   e. linking individual views to develop a common view and to guide groups in shaping that view into a dynamic and motivating vision

130

Facilitating development of the Vision sometimes means pointing group members toward assets and resources the organization already owns but hasn't considered using with future opportunities. A good visioning process helps surface and connect private thoughts about options in a supportive but public environment.

Linked with the ideas of others, previously unspoken thoughts about a Vision for the future can be voiced, analyzed and reinforced. They take shape with real potential. Options for achieving the Vision, with shared awareness of competitor activities, with new opportunities for partnering, and with access to previously undeveloped resources enable ideas that might have been discounted or ignored in other settings. The ideas become not only workable but very achievable. Group synergy in all these areas leads to acceptance of new directions and changes within an increasingly linked, expanded, and energized stakeholder group.

Lofty or Lose It

The Bell Curve of attitudes towards major changes described in *Chapter 3 — Involvement* also demonstrates the impact of a less-than-lofty, uninspiring Vision (see *Figure 6.3*). Top-level leaders usually yield to the fear that the unconfirmed majority (in reality, probably a small minority) will not support the plan. They water down the energizing Vision, believing that they will then get 100% support and commitment to the new, watered down Vision. But the opposite always happens.

The watered-down plan doesn't inspire the most energetic, creative leaders and supporters. Their involvement and attitude changes to half-hearted or even grumbling support. Next, the 60% majority who usually jump on board when they see strong

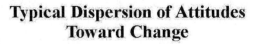

**Typical Dispersion of Attitudes
Toward Change**

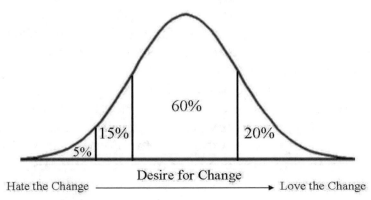

60%

15%

20%

5%

Desire for Change

Hate the Change ⟶ Love the Change

Figure 6.3

movement by trusted leaders join in the now half-hearted attitude. The worst effect of watered-down visions, however, is that they do not help to achieve the desired result — the plan will not be effective.

Safe, obvious visions inspire and motivate no one.[5] They do not increase group unity beyond the current state. They are not worth the time they take to develop. Because the ensuing plan will not be effective, "safe" visions lead to negative feelings about leadership and strategic planning. They lead people to disengage rather than support.

Theopolis Enterprises

Theopolis Enterprises became a house divided because of conflicting visions. At first, it seemed like a great idea: merge six entities related to helping people into one major organization; cut the administrative costs and maximize the people and financial resources available for programs. A new executive administrator was chosen, David Jordan, with direct responsibility for service programs: food and shelter,

AIDs ministry, immigration assistance, and family counseling. Amy Spelt became deputy administrator for social justice, which included responsibility for program development and community and government relations. The social justice advocacy issues were myriad and frequently very controversial.

A new Board of Directors, comprised of members representing all the constituencies of the previous solo organizations, was selected for their knowledge of each service area and for their influence and connections with the general community, education, healthcare, and government stakeholders. Formation of the Board and merger of operations and resources all went well.

Staff and volunteers were very committed to Theopolis and became even more enthusiastic about its potential with the merger/reorganization. They all saw increased opportunities, beneficial linkages, and expanding programs. Board meetings were now upbeat, fun, and very productive — until proposals for new directions and increased funding requests for expanding programs began to show up on the Board's agenda.

The battles began and exploded. Board members who represented the service programs were nervous and concerned. They feared their strongest funders would oppose the controversial positions and strong public messages being proposed for the social justice program.

Board members realized they needed a strong Vision to help steer their decisions, consistent with their basic values. It became clear that beyond the basic value of desiring to help humankind, there was huge diversity in the values and in the directions represented on the Board. Service program advocates proposed softer, safer messages, and more generally acceptable public positions and messages.

That less-provocative approach to public mes-sages didn't sit well with the social justice-focused Board members. They felt they couldn't accomplish their Mission or satisfy their funders without visibly taking positions and advocating directions that were more publicly controversial. They needed a Vision that would communicate that message. Without it, they couldn't inspire their constituencies.

In the end, work towards a meaningful Vision led to splitting the new organization in two — each with a dynamic Vision that led to major growth, great public visibility, and constituent respect in both areas. They both flourished.

Fed Ex didn't say, "We will work toward getting it to them the next day"; they said, "They will get it the next day." That was a powerful picture and direction that motivated everyone and that everyone could see, from the front-desk customer-intake people, to couriers, to dispatch teams, to marketing and sales people, and to IT, logistics, supply-chain coordination, accounting and quality-control teams. From that simple, seven-word Vision, all depart-ments knew what to plan and knew what strategies they needed to develop. All staff, managers, board members, and vendors could understand that Vision. They each developed their pieces of the plan to accomplish it.

Most organizations will need more than seven words to paint a powerful picture that everyone can see. The key is that the Vision must be focused only on one primary, clear view of a future significantly altered from today. That picture cannot be split to satisfy different constituencies. There can be two or more major directions, but the directions must be unified and be consistent with one central, unique Vision. If these directions diverge, they will cause problems with marketing, financing, branding, and personnel resources. The result is either a split personality or a nebulous cloud.

Leading Groups to See What They Haven't Yet Imagined

The Vision Rule

Safe, obvious Visions don't inspire and they don't increase commitment. They do not increase group unity beyond the current state.

Truly challenging Visions do inspire and lead to breakthrough accomplishments that can rapidly catapult organizations forward, to leapfrog competitors and far out-distance them.

If it isn't visionary, it isn't a Vision!

One leader can build a wonderful Vision and can convince close supporters and some others of its potential. The problem is that many others will see the future differently. Those other visions may be less of a stretch, safer. Other vision proponents may have less exposure to outside trends and forces. Or, they may see difficulties ahead for the leader's proposed Vision without knowing the paths to resolving them — they don't know the countervailing factors and the available resources.

That's why group development of the Vision is so critical. There are three critical questions to ask about Visions:

1. How can leaders develop lofty visions that will inspire and be embraced by everyone in the organization?

2. How can leaders learn the true feelings and attitudes of the people in their organizations, develop actions that result in change, and move ahead with assurance in new directions?

3. How can leaders minimize the potential for dissension, change skeptical attitudes and thus generate support for new directions?

The answer to all three questions is the same: by using an effective, tiered and cross-organizational group process to research, brainstorm, plan, and implement.

Rules for Successful Strategic Planning

1. Don't confuse strategic with operations planning, as many do. Strategic planning often gets tainted with the operations planning brush. Strategic planning should be simple, fun, inspiring, and exciting.

2. Realize that Vision, not Mission, is the core driver of a Strategic Plan. The Vision statement differs greatly from the Mission; it isn't even close. Without an exciting, unifying and inspiring Vision statement, implementation of the strategic plan can become a laborious, contentious process.

3. Take the fear factor out of strategic planning as much as possible. Make it safe for people to be daring. Reward their risk-taking ideas with public kudos. Link specific individuals to innovations and give credit wherever and whenever possible.

4. Assess and assure a strong infrastructure. Good infrastructure is very reassuring; it enables people to see the roads to success, to see the internal resources, to understand how plans developed within their departments will connect with others to make the strategies happen. It helps them to *believe* in the Plan.

5. Build good communication networks and tools, just for the strategic-planning process. This will permit everyone to see, as quickly as possible, that pieces are coming together within other departments and to think about the effect on their work. Good communication tools will speed organization unity. It helps them to *feel* success and keep on working when the going gets tough.

Strategic planning for major changes and new directions is a very different planning process than that used for implementing technical or operational system changes. Seventy-five percent of the benefits gained from strategic planning are in the changes created during the process for the organization itself: changes to the culture, structure, environment, communications systems, human relations, and values. Wherever changes are needed, strategic planning is the most effective and all-encompassing place to start.

The greatest challenge in accomplishing any organizational goal is that typically people aren't linked adequately, processes and systems don't provide the tools they need, and people don't have the goal clarity needed to understand the role of their department. People need to fully understand their own roles and their context within the greater organization goal. Everyone within each department should be able to see the linkages between their department's and their own assigned strategies and action plans and the Vision. Each individual can then effectively develop his/her own specific action plan and steps to link with the strategies of others.

Once leaders look at the organization from a macro level, through an effective strategic planning process with an inspiring Vision at its core, the solution or needed change becomes obvious. A good strategic planning process enables leaders to communicate with people in a meaningful and linked way across departments and at different levels, to ask questions and *really listen*. Once the problem or goal is determined, deeply and expansively, leaders can focus on revising the organizational structure, appropriately linking teams, and improving systems and processes to promote collaboration needed for achieving successful change.

The most creative initiative or growth plan will soon falter and fail without sound infrastructure to support it. Strategic planning is the most effective way to start towards achieving a goal, but sound infrastructure is the framework that supports solid and sustainable implementation.

Chapter 7:
Infrastructure
Building Foundations to Withstand Storms

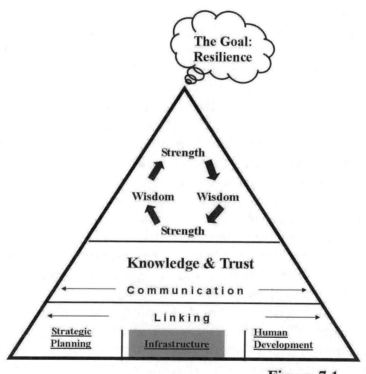

Figure 7.1

SuperPerform

SuperPerform was a VAR (value-added reseller), one of Oregon's fastest growing start-up companies. They reached $400M in sales in five years. Their product development team was making great strides. New customer growth was on a steep upward trend. At that point, SuperPerform developed major problems. Top-level managers, but not C-Suite officers, worried because Customer Service couldn't keep up with complaints. Their products broke down at an increasing rate. As a result, SuperPerform lost customers almost as fast as the sales team replaced them. And 20% of production went towards replacement of returned products.

The problem wasn't people, although people were blamed. The problem was inadequate infrastructure, which hampered collaboration and communication between departments. Consultants and managers assessed the situation and developed plans for changes in quality control, production, and customer-service processes that would improve product and service performance fairly quickly.

The managers were very excited, optimistic, and motivated to make the changes immediately, even when it added to their individual workloads. Work on these changes would take resources away from sales, marketing, and product development, but the costs were low and would be more than recovered within the next quarter.

C-Suite officers vetoed the plan. They wanted all resources focused on increasing sales and product development — even more rapid growth — to impress their funders. They thought increased sales would cover the lost customers. Sadly, needlessly, SuperPerform continued to lose customers at an increasing rate. Sales could not keep up with the customer losses. The Company folded one year later.

Often, when greater growth or a major change stalls, leaders and team members don't know why. They see only symptoms — a key department falling behind or delivering poor-quality work. They don't see true causes. These are hidden in the subterranean level, in the organization's un-exposed skeleton— that is, in its Infrastructure.

Infrastructure is the critical link between all parts of an organization — the most overlooked, undercapitalized and undervalued part. Thus, it is the cause of more problems and more failures of growth initiatives than any other component. If a company's infrastructure doesn't function effec-tively, or if various parts function unevenly, none of the other pieces — operations, sales, finance — can function at their desired levels.

Infrastructure Holds It Together

Infrastructure is the skeleton that supports the organization. By its very nature, infrastructure is invisible and (except for computer-related compo-nents) intangible. Although certain systems (e.g., inventory and accounts receivable) are considered important, no one sees interfaces between them. Most infrastructure components, like the reporting structure or the processes for linking knowledge across departments, are completely invisible — and sometimes completely undefined, too.

Yet these systems and processes — the organi-zation's infrastructure — are what enable people to perform efficiently and in sync, or prevent them from doing so. Infrastructure is made up of:

- *Organization reporting structure:* the roles, responsibilities, and job descriptions that define the relationships across departments and the linking of roles within departments.

- *Information and communication systems* that support all operations and functions and link them with one another effectively.

- *Processes and policies* that identify, link, and document tasks and activities to assure efficiency and consistency, reduce redundancy, and ensure quality performance.

Optimum performance, profitability, and adherence to the organization's mission all depend upon effective infrastructure. Performance improvement tools (e.g., Balanced Scorecard or Lean), aggressive strategic plans, or changes in management *cannot* compensate for inadequate infrastructure. Good infrastructure enables strong internal communications, so knowledge flows freely and on time. It facilitates meaningful individual involvement and effective teams.

Organizations that have high-level humanitarian values and social goals frequently dismiss business structures and processes as unimportant — or worse, they view structures, policies, and processes as distractions to achieving their Mission-focused values and objectives. So, ironically, the higher the social goals, the weaker internal communication and effective use of human capital and financial resources tend to be.

Silent Spring grew with minimal attention to infrastructure. It almost imploded.

Silent Spring, Part I
Silent Spring, a specialty education-focused entity, has an excellent reputation for outstanding teaching. The organization, however, had major challenges. Both the CEO and the CFO were under heavy stress and also had significant health problems, which

were no doubt exacerbated by a poor management reporting structure, minimal formal operating processes, and inadequate information systems. As the organization structure expanded to 18 operating and administrative departments, all reporting through the CFO to the CEO, its opportunities and problems also grew Because of Silent Spring's national visibility and their reputation for high-quality programs, their enrollment escalated; they were bursting at the seams. They had significant growth plans, including a major capital campaign for construction of several new buildings on their campus. They realized that they could not move forward without also making significant improvements to their internal operations structure.

Several glaring symptoms triggered their desire to fix the organizational problems. They recognized that they had made bad hiring decisions. Employee lawsuits occurred regularly, which resulted in expensive settlements, creating many distractions when Silent Spring most needed to focus on growth and development. The major underlying problem was inadequate personnel infrastructure, including inadequate hiring procedures, insufficient orientation and training, not enough supervision or feedback, and no performance reviews or documentation of personnel achievements and deficiencies.

Because there were no performance measures or clear job definitions, there were frequent conflicts over responsibility areas. Many important tasks weren't accomplished because everyone assumed someone else was responsible. Difficult tasks were easy to ignore; finger-pointing was constant. Few people ever went the extra mile, and if they did, their efforts weren't recognized. Some people were overloaded to the point of exhaustion but didn't delegate for fear the jobs wouldn't get done — and all too often, that is just what happened. Significant time, dollars, and emotional stress were spent on hiring, initial training, and attorneys.

At the same time, the organization was growing due to the reputation of the education program: high-quality leaders and teachers, wonderful values and philosophy, cutting-edge programs, and accolades from those who hired the graduates.

While the education division was flourishing, however, other programs and activities suffered due to inadequate attention. As a result, non-education activities drained time and money rather than contributing to growth.

Infrastructure Improvement — An Iterative, Phased Process

Infrastructure can be assessed and strengthened as part of another initiative; for example, as part of a reorganization, merger, new product line, or system transition. Or changes to any major component, segment, or piece of infrastructure can be made independently as problems or needs emerge.

Either way, the road to successful infrastructure improvement proceeds in stages:

1. Fully understand the problem (Assessment)

2. Develop alternatives and select the solution (Design)

3. Develop implementation plan and monitoring process (Execution)

People *involvement* is the key to assuring successful and sustainable solutions. As the change process moves through each phase, the number of people involved should increase.

People involvement is important for all change projects, as described in *Chapter 4 — Real Involvement*, but for infrastructure projects in particular, the only way to effectively build improvements is to have the people who will use it build it. They know the systems and issues best. They can most quickly identify gaps and overlaps in operations. Guided by the basic principles and steps described below and facilitated by the consultants and managers who understand iterative process and know how to listen, those responsible for implementation can effectively design infrastructure improvements.

The Pathway to Improvement[1] — Part I

Three phases — Assessment, Design, Execution — each include the same basic steps designed to be iterative and overlapping. This maximizes targeted group involvement and efficiency (see *Appendix* for a summary). The goal in each step is to:

- reinforce knowledge gained in the previous step

- move forward toward design and execution with

    o increasing knowledge
    o alternatives that have been exposed to and tested by an increasing number of stakeholders
    o stronger belief in the solution by all participants.

For very large or complex entities, consider expanding the steps to include additional overlapping phases. For simple improvements or very small organizations, you might compress the steps.

*Phase One – **Assess** Current Situation*

1. Collect information about current status

2. Summarize and analyze the issues (Result: the Assessment Report)

3. Discuss and debate/inform and involve stakeholders

*Phase Two – **Design** Solutions*

4. Collect information to develop alternatives

5. Summarize and analyze information (Result: the Design Report)

6. Develop alternatives; select solution(s)

*Phase Three – **Execute** Solutions*

7. Research and design implementation process and structure

8. Summarize implementation plan; design tools

9. Implement, monitor, and improve

Phase One – Assess Current Situation
Step 1. Collect Information about Current Status
When growth stalls or change initiatives get mired, leaders typically ask consultants for help, saying things like, "The Finance Department doesn't work effectively" or "Our Sales Department people are not helping us get where we want to go," but usually, these people are not at fault. The problem is that people aren't linked together adequately, processes

and systems don't provide the tools they need, or they don't have the goal/strategy clarity they need in order to perform well.

Unless people understand their roles completely, initiatives will fail. The Vision must be clearly translated into objectives and goals, then detailed into specific strategies for each department, so each can see the links between their assigned strategies and the Vision. Effective infrastructure then facilitates each department's ability to accomplish its own assigned strategies. Without good infrastructure to support it, the most creative initiative, growth plan, or important change will falter and fail.

Whether successfully implementing initiatives or solving performance problems, the first step is to clearly *understand* the issue and its environment. Core questions below in **Box 7.1** start that process.

Issue Assessment - First, Learn the Environment:

- What organizational values relate to the issue or initiative?
- What is the organizational structure of departments and of people within departments who are involved with the issue (both directly and indirectly)? How do they relate to the issue/initiative?
- What essential information do people share? Where does the information come from and in what format? Where does it go?
- Empowering motivations: What messages do leaders send (spoken and implied) about the importance of the initiative?
- Are there *documented* processes and policies that will affect accomplishment of the initiative?

Box 7.1

Don't be tempted to shirk these basic environmental questions above or core questions below. A thorough assessment of the situation leads to high-quality analysis of alternatives and points the way to most of the solutions, especially in the area of typically invisible, undervalued infrastructure.

Far too often, organizations move to implement solutions after performing only superficial assessments, which typically focus on the most obvious, most visible causes. Usually, these obvious causes are only symptoms, not really true causes. The result is that the solutions are only bandaids. They do not effectively solve the problem and are not sustainable. The assessment was so superficial that it didn't get to the core issues!

Getting to the Real Issues — Core Questions:

Once you have gathered information at a macro issue level (**Box 7.1**), you can develop more detailed facts about the specific deficiencies you have identified.

Boxes 7.2, 7.3, and **7.4** outline key questions for you to research and answer related to each of the three major infrastructure component areas:

1. Reporting, linking, responsibility structures

2. Processes and policies

3. Information and communications systems

Be prepared to add additional questions based on the responses you receive during the Environmental Assessment questioning in **Box 7.1** on the previous page and also as you obtain answers to the core questions for each area in **Boxes 7.2, 7.3,** and **7.4**.

Core Questions: Reporting, Linking, & Responsibility Structures:

1. What is the Mission/purpose of the organization? How is it accomplished? What are the major product/service categories to accomplish the Mission?
2. What is the current Vision? What are the major organizational Goals for the next three years?
3. How does the configuration of the major operations divisions/departments relate to the Mission/purpose and the current Vision and Goals? Are they consistent with the Mission and Goals?
4. Are there major divisions/departments that correspond to the resources needed (e.g., people, equipment, funding, outside service providers, development/ innovation, outside supporters) to accomplish the Mission and the current Vision and Goals?
5. If there is a major issue or challenge, how are the related departments structured and how are their structures linked to one another?
6. To what extent is this structure framework documented in charts? To what extent are the charts visible to all stakeholders?
7. Do job descriptions exist for every position? Does the description include the role, responsibilities, and reporting links above and below the position as well as the links across the organization? Are the descriptions summarized for and available to appropriate related stakeholders?

Box 7.2

Core Questions: Processes and Policies

1. What activities are contained within each department, both operational and resource departments? Are the objectives and key activities within each department summarized, documented and visible to all related stakeholders?
2. Are the processes and policies for all activities within the organization documented, including resource departments, (e.g., human resources, quality control, purchasing)?
3. Are the *links between processes* documented across departments, (i.e., how does work come into the department from every other department and where does it go)?
4. Is the process documentation reviewed and reassessed regularly to assure awareness of changes and to determine areas for improvement?
5. Is the documentation and assessment done by teams and reviewed by representatives from affected departments and groups?

Box 7.3

Core Questions: Information and Communications Systems

1. What information comes into each department – from each department (operations and resource) and from outside? In what form (e.g. software system, cloud, hard copy, verbal) does it enter and in what configuration/format?

Box 7.4

**Core Questions: Information and
Communications Systems,** Continued

   2. Is the information received within each department consistent and efficient to the extent
possible?

   3. What structured communication vehicles exist for
sharing and discussing changes to processes
and policies, organizational initiatives, organization structure, and position changes for their
implications within and across departments? Are
the vehicles utilized and effective?

Box 7.4

Getting the Best Answers — Use Interviews
Probing interviews produce the most valuable answers; broadcast questionnaires and surveys provide
only superficial ones. Focus groups are beneficial
for other purposes, but interviews give the greatest
insight into important, often hidden, issues.

Typically, when leaders perceive a problem, the
"solution" they see is actually a symptom; the root
problem is almost always deeper and broader.
Investigating, analyzing, and then digging around to
find the root problem produces treasures much
greater than the superficial gems everyone believes
are the causes and solutions.

To find these treasures, the interview process
must be carefully designed, interviewees purposefully selected, and interviews skillfully conducted.
Thorough interviews, especially in the critically
important Assessment phase, are key to effective
infrastructure improvements.

First, start with the CEO and a few core leaders
from upper management to gain a broad view of the
issue. Interview this core group to both refine the

interview questions and to identify other important interviewees. The interviewee list should typically cross departments, go deeper into the organization, and include some perceived dissidents in order to obtain different perspectives.

Use additional interviews and process maps and also review typical related reports and schedules to identify other problem areas. Prioritize each problem you identify — is it an isolated one or does it impact other departments? Few real problems are isolated, but most problem/change assessments stop at the simplest, most obvious levels. "Keys to Effective Interviews" in *Chapter 8 — People Focus* gives you tips on conducting effective interviews.

Meaningful assessment is the most important step to successful change, but it is most frequently skipped or given minimal attention. Leaders typically think they know the issues and understand the problem. They immediately take action, moving ahead on what is, in reality, only a symptom. They almost never get to the root cause and may exacerbate the problem or cause new ones. Steps that stem from a perceptive assessment are faster and more likely to produce a sustainable change. A good assessment also reveals related problems that, untreated, might lead to future crises.

Step 2. Summarize and Analyze the Issues
How you organize the recorded information is key to effective analysis and design of effective solutions. Many interviewers simply summarize all interviewee comments and then add their conclusions in the summary report. Instead, sort the documented comments by topic and include them verbatim in the report. This approach accelerates the analysis process, enables much more focused solutions, and makes reports more interesting and more useful.

Seeing the details of other people's observations, individual by individual (coded for confidentiality), publicly documented in a written report, helps to validate, reinforce, or negate the readers' own perceptions. Reading others' thoughts alongside their own comments or views about causes, implications, cures, etc., also helps leaders and workers to see problems and solutions from other viewpoints in a very credible way.

Summary statements, such as "75% of people say...," which are used in most reports, don't carry as much weight or provide enough information. The percentages are also suspect due to stakeholders' perceptions about the consultant's or manager's biased interpretations of interviewees' comments. Grouping individual comments, listed by category of need, issue, or solution and also by stakeholder group, helps to clearly display the commonalities and differences. It helps to define the issues better and builds unity.

When people read their own exact words in a report, they assume that others' are accurately recorded, too. This adds credibility to both the report and the process. People are suspicious about statistics that collect survey data because of real and perceived flaws in the manner of collection and analysis.

The method described above, of sorting interview documentation in ways that preserve individual comments and enable people to see patterns, makes solutions easier to find, more accurate, and more sustainable; it also makes subsequent solutions much more credible. The process of grouping responses and quoting individual comments also makes the Assessment process more transparent and builds trust, which helps teams working on the next steps.

Step 3. Discuss and Debate — Inform and Involve Stakeholders

After the Assessment Report is completed, involve people from throughout the organization. Begin by distributing the report and deciding how to discuss and supplement it. Collect ideas, reactions, and suggestions for future consideration and research. Be sure to select an experienced and skilled facilitator. See **Box 7.5** for selection criteria.

Also use these sessions to:

- Inform stakeholders about next steps and ways that they might be involved

- Watch for potential planning/implementation team leaders

Step 3 increases stakeholders' trust in the process and belief in their leaders' commitment to involve them. The result will be greater acceptance and more sincere adoption of eventual solutions.

Select Skilled Facilitators

Choose facilitators who will be respected by internal and external stakeholders as guides and who:

- Will be immediately perceived as objective
- Are skilled in seeing both "big picture" issues and micro ones
- Have deep experience with both operations and resource departments and at all organization levels, from C-Suite to basic-level production
- Understand organizational behavior and structures and how people behave within them.

Box 7.5

Phase Two – Design Solutions

The Design phase starts with collecting information to develop several alternative solutions, involving stakeholders at every step of the process. The more meaningfully you involve stakeholders, the better the solutions will be and the more readily people will accept them.

Step 4. Collect Information to Develop Alternatives

After Assessment, collect more detailed information before choosing a solution. Go to those individuals with detailed knowledge of the areas that will be affected by the issues. For infrastructure improvement projects, that means people from throughout the organization.

The tendency in most organizations is for a core group to simply debate obvious possibilities for solutions, using their own experience, exposure, and opinions. Discussions frequently occur without adequate research and analysis of alternatives to guide the process.

The pitfall of using a small core group to collect additional information and to develop solutions is that, without a good process and additional outside knowledge, the personal biases and perceptions of those who were most obviously involved in the issue in the past get too much weight. The core group gets bogged down by their personal experiences; it is difficult for them to hear and assess alternatives. Their solutions are therefore suspect even before they announce or begin to implement them. The potential for resolving issues is reduced before problem-solving even starts.

So make sure to get solid evidence about the area that needs improving — the more specific, the better. That means preliminary research about history and impact of the issue and collection of existing tools (appropriate policies and processes, diagrams and process maps, sample reports and charts).

Use of an outside consultant to facilitate this information-collection process can also help assure that biases and personal perceptions of internal consultants don't overwhelm the discussions and prevent open consideration of new ideas.

Involve People

The first step to solutions is to increase knowledge about the implications and scope of the issues, while providing more ideas for possible solutions. The more stakeholders you involve, the broader the organizational awareness and understanding of the project will be. As you meet with involved participants, constantly acknowledge and consider their ideas. Thank them for their contributions.

Use focus groups, more interviews, and surveys on specific points to reach many more people. More specifically:

- Draw targeted questions for discussion and surveys from the Assessment Report to inform and to validate the Report findings.

- Collect detailed examples of the issue's implications and scope and thoughts about the alternative solutions.

- Select a knowledgeable team to supervise the information/research process and collection of the results.

- Here again, an outside consultant can help assure the objectivity, diversity and completeness of the information-gathering process.

Skimping on these steps may *seem* to save time, but it never does. Only a comprehensive, inclusive problem-solving process produces a sustainable solution, one that builds buy-in throughout the organization. It also results in less complaining and finger-pointing later.

Collect Evidence — Examples and Tools
Most organizations don't document their processes or have basic process maps. Leaders don't realize that *process maps* for resource departments — such as human resources, finance, planning, and IT — help to improve knowledge and efficiency not only in those departments but in all other departments as well. Process maps immediately lead to greater efficiency, productivity, and error reduction. Their benefits outweigh the time it takes to produce them, many times over. Employees at organizations with process maps bring them to every meeting and brainstorming session. When discussing issues and changes, they pull out the maps and point to a particular process area, saying "Here it is. Here is the problem I am talking about! We can fix this!"

When *organization reporting/responsibility charts* (org charts) are available within organizations, they usually exist only at a macro level, displaying only major operating departments or divisions. Charts are typically distributed only to managers, executives, and Board members. Leaders do not realize how valuable org charts are to others throughout the organization.

Org charts are especially helpful when groups meet to plan or problem-solve, because they show lines of authority and linkages across departments and sub-groups. Many companies find that when they first document reporting relationships, both within and across departments, people experience amazing "aha!" moments that trigger big improvements to communication and collaboration — for both problem-solving and planning.

Improvement teams should prepare org charts, focusing especially on all areas that may be affected by the planned infrastructure changes.

Unfortunately, organizations don't often prepare *performance measures* for infrastructure areas or develop *benchmarks* for infrastructure improvement projects. If they do exist for areas to be developed/ improved, collect them. If they don't, create them. These valuable tools facilitate timely completion of projects by boosting accountability and enhancing communication.

Infrastructure tools (for example, process and system maps, documented company policies, org charts, benchmarks, and performance measures) are valuable in developing goals for improvement and in measuring progress towards those goals. They also help plan and assure organization unity. The result is more rapid growth and effective performance.

Step 5. Summarize and Analyze Information (Result: the **Design** *Report)*
By this stage, many more organization stakeholders will have added clarity about the direction needed, greater precision in the areas on which to focus, and more understanding about potential negative reverberations. The core planning team will have collected a significant amount of documentation: examples that clearly demonstrate the issues, areas identified for improvement, useful tools available for the implementation phase, and opportunities targeted for future study. This valuable information will reinforce the need for and benefits from change. It will also provide clear direction for improvement,

enable advance planning to remove roadblocks, and prevent problems that might later derail implementation.

Step 5 requires a careful, skilled review and analysis of the evidence collected. Because of the macro, linked view required to accomplish this effectively, Step 5 can only be completed by a small cohort — the consultant/project manager assisted by a few selected leaders. The objective is to present the new information — the preliminary Design Report — in ways that will enable team members and other readers to understand the implications and messages in an impactful and persuasive way. Summaries are important, but only when backed by verbatim statements and documents that prove the accuracy and significance of the distilled knowledge and suggested directions.

Later, at Step 6, implementation teams begin to own the project. This ownership assures successful implementation and sustainable results. The best way to assure consistent good results from teams is to incorporate accountability processes into every infrastructure improvement project.

To assure accountability, once the information above is collected into a meaningful and easily readable Design Report with a clear conclusion and major change directions, preparation for design/ implementation teams can begin in this order:

1. Define and then select the teams. Use the Design Report to determine the scope and complexity of the topics and structures; this will determine the number and size of the teams. Select team members from a variety of departments because the resulting implementation steps and tools will be used by most, if not all, segments of the organization.

2. Develop an efficient process for the teams to follow. Teams need roadmaps to aid them in developing the solution, implementation recommendations, and tools. A strong planning structure and process helps to assure successful, timely, and efficient progress. The most important processes to develop for teams are in **Box 7.6.**

Process Guides to Prepare for Teams

- Standard *process for developing recommendations*, including adequate research and consideration of alternative steps and tools, pros and cons, costs, and resource needs
- Standard *format for presenting* recommendations
- Standard *process for approval* of recommendations
- Reasonable *timelines* for completion and implementation of recommendations

Box 7.6

---

3. Design reporting formats and systems for the teams. Accountability/reporting tools should be prepared and in place before the teams begin Implementation steps. These tools will help assure that projects will be completed on time and on budget. Using these change tools for every infrastructure improvement project will also strengthen accountability within the organization's culture. The most important tools to facilitate accountability within the teams are shown in **Box 7.7**.

Provide Accountability Tools

1. Establish clear assignments, responsibilities, timelines, deadlines, and benchmarks for progress.
2. Develop **visible** processes and consistent timing for reporting progress on the project so that everyone within the organization can see progress.
3. Use established internal communication tools and processes. This will help awareness of the infrastructure improvement projects and also promote the importance and regular use of established communication processes (including update meetings, internal newsletters, intranet, etc.).

Box 7.7

The next steps in Infrastructure Improvement — further developing the solution steps and also designing, effecting, and monitoring execution — all require meaningful involvement and empowerment of the organization's people. The assessment, the organizational/departmental structure, and process tools are good instruments to use in accomplishing successful change, but it is people who use these instruments. Focus on *people* is the key to fixing every problem and successfully accomplishing every opportunity.

Respectful treatment and sincere caring about people, at every level of the organization, ensures that all challenges will be met smoothly and effect-tively. *Chapter 8 — People Focus* describes how working to implement Infrastructure improvements does more than increase productivity and lead to successful change projects. People focus helps to build organizational resilience.

Infrastructure — Undervalued and Neglected Resource

Departments are frequently blamed for failures that actually stem from the inadequate infrastructure. When people are blamed for infrastructure problems, individuals or work groups blame themselves and become frustrated as they try, and then fail, to complete their assigned activities on schedule. Others within the organization blame the failing individuals or groups who, in turn, lose confidence in themselves and fall further behind. The downward cycle jeopardizes successful completion or sustainability of the change and negatively affects the whole organization's resilience.

Greater focus on infrastructure ALWAYS results in improved profitability, efficiency, capacity, and employee morale. Minimized infrastructure has the opposite effect. The key is to focus on improvement of infrastructure, not on cutting its resources. The objective should be to increase the capability and effectiveness of infrastructure so it supports all departments and contributes to growth.

As we saw with *SuperPerform* and *Silent Spring*, when infrastructure areas are not visible or valued, IT IS IMPOSSIBLE for other areas to function optimally. With strong focus on infrastructure, even governmental entities are able to excel at effective and entrepreneurial performance. *TriMet Light Rail* proved it.

TriMet Light Rail

Tuck Wilson and Neil McFarlane were the Executive Director and Director of Operations for TriMet Light Rail, Oregon's highly regarded mass-transit system. They proved that strong, effective infrastructure enables an organization to maximize productivity and profitability, even at a large government entity.

TriMet's Light Rail division became renowned for its ability to deliver billion-dollar construction projects on time and under budget.

Tuck and Neil are two of the most entrepreneurial and innovative governmental leaders with whom I have worked. Emotionally intelligent leaders, who understand good process and good communication, they made TriMet Light Rail the efficient, effective operation it is. They constantly worked to make it even better.

Identifying the Need: *As TriMet Light Rail grew, doing more and bigger light-rail installations, Tuck and Neil realized that it was getting harder to assure high-quality and high-level customer service — both internally and externally. Unnecessary mistakes and slowdowns started occurring on their highly successful Westside Project. They wanted to find out why the mistakes occurred and retool their processes to find and correct the problem areas.*

They did this while they were designing and planning their next big project, Interstate. Interstate was in a much denser population area than Westside and was likely to encounter many more complex issues. They didn't want to wait until the emerging problems became crises. They didn't want to wait until the problems started affecting their time or budget. Instead, they brought in outside consultants to objectively assess the processes and help the department managers define problem areas and develop solutions.

The assessment stage included review of critical infrastructure areas:

- *Procurement*

- *Project Control*

- *Organization and Staffing*

- *Management*

The assessment showed that improvements were needed in major areas:

1. *Communication — better processes and more tools to improve cross-organizational dialogue and information flow.*

2. *Documentation — standard guidelines and better processes to assure compliance with documentation requirements and to improve efficiency and quality service.*

3. *Coordination — improved processes to assure greater coordination and minimize crises across the organization.*

4. *Information Systems – standardized software with greater capacity for linking in order to increase efficiency; standard reports with consistent formats and terminology; and more multi-purpose reports to enhance dialogue and minimize duplication and errors.*

Steps to Greater Success: *The TriMet Light Rail division took steps in all these areas and went on to achieve another on-time, on-budget completion of a very complex project. The new unified teams were even more effective due to the enhanced infrastructure. They were able to accomplish more and solve tougher problems more effectively and efficiently.*

As a result of these changes, both internal and external stakeholders became more unified. TriMet Light Rail already had a philosophy that helped to link and maximize the performance of their project teams: Tuck and Neil both believed in treating their vendors as important customers — an unheard-of philosophy, in my experience. The Light Rail division was attentive to vendors, completed commitments on time for their vendors as well as for their internal and external customers, and dedicated adequate resources (time and assigned personnel) to working with them. They treated vendors as important parts of their team.

TriMet Light Rail leaders were very fair with their vendors but they also had very high expectations. In fee negotiations, for example, they pushed for a good, but fair, price. They didn't leave vendors feeling resentful about unfair, harsh terms. As a result, vendors were committed, loved working with Light Rail, and wanted *to give more than expected. The very best vendors, who ordinarily didn't want to work with government entities, competed heavily to work for Light Rail. These vendors gave TriMet Light Rail their best people, not their least-experienced, lowest-priced ones as they did with less desirable clients. Their philosophy of treating vendors as respected team members, along with established processes for implementing that philosophy, also added significantly to TriMet Light Rail's ability to accomplish projects on time and under budget.*

Strong Infrastructure Assures Successful Change and Builds Resilience

Speed doesn't lead to greater success, but greater effectiveness does. Improvements that enhance the effectiveness of teams and individuals in operations activities will also lead to their greater ability to respond, whenever needed, with the best possible solution for each challenge or opportunity. Think of it as the "no-huddle offense" of great football teams or the fast responses of the best soccer teams. Effective companies don't need a huddle; they *act with a collective heartbeat, as one.*

Ultimately, infrastructure is all about people and planning. Good infrastructure requires that people work together; it takes time to improve, but it can make a huge difference in the quality of work life, in efficiency, and in the quality completion of critical initiatives. Working to improve infrastructure takes time away from accomplishing ordinary tasks but almost immediately creates efficiencies and more productive accomplishment of goals. Work on infrastructure is one of the best investments in its future that an organization can make, because it enables the Ability to change successfully and to sustain the change. It is the base of the formula to create Resilience, as *Figure 7.2* displays.

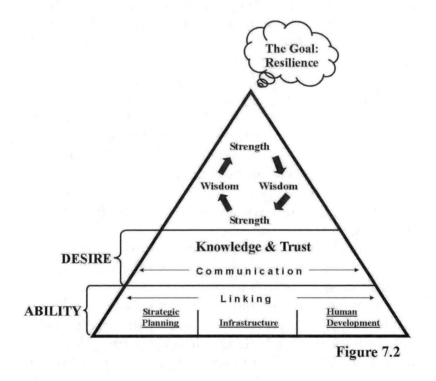

Figure 7.2

Chapter 8: People Focus

Creating an Environment Where People Can Grow and Thrive

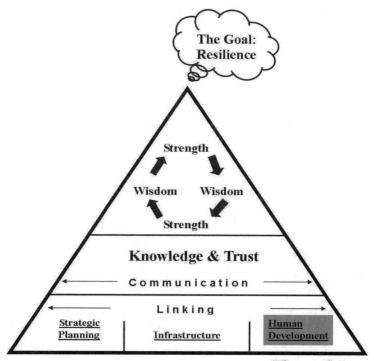

Figure 8.1

*T*riMet Light Rail's treatment of vendors as important customers and as team members, described in *Chapter 7 — Infrastructure*, is an example of a culture that enables people — all stakeholders — to constantly work at their best. This type of culture creates a Resilient organization. *TriMet Light Rail* is a recognized, well-established force in successfully completing projects because of its inclusive, people-focused culture.

Cultures that meaningfully involve people lead to more resilient organizations, even in traditionally bureaucratic, governmental ones. This type of culture also benefits not-for-profit organizations, but their typically minimal infrastructure works against people focus. *Mercurial Academy* is a good example.

Mercurial Academy, Part 2

Mercurial Academy, the nationally renowned school introduced in Chapter 6 — Strategic Vision, *was successful in growing revenues in spite of a double crisis: the Great Recession and a scandal. Jo Ross, the new Event Manager, developed a plan to go after new markets and build a strong team. She figured that they'd lost many of their usual donors and should replace them from new groups. She knew that challenges require taking risks: new strategies developed and implemented by people with hands-on knowledge of the market, motivated by energizing goals, reinforced by documented processes and good communication systems.*

Jo also learned about the organization's culture before she arrived, particularly about the Development Department and the Event Teams. There was little sharing and little communication across the organization and the department. New strategies were not accepted warmly, including changes to the standard Event formula. As a result, the usual fall-

back response to challenges was to simply reduce the Goal and Mercurial's operating budget.

Jo recognized that failure was a possibility but believed in the strength of the organization's Mission and in the potential for success if changes were made to the Event planning, organization structure, and marketing process.

An expanded Event Team shared ideas, designed micro-events sponsored by volunteers to motivate leaders in the new market areas, and raised *the goal to energize both Team members and volunteers. The result was that Mercurial beat its previous fund-raising record, in a year of horrible crisis, through working together as One on a significant change.*

Becoming One, working with a *collective heart-beat*, is about enabling stakeholders to constantly work at their best. Knowing that they are part of a strong team and feeling personally empowered to respond to challenges, individuals take action when they see a problem or potential for improvement.

Biggest Barriers to Successful Change

Motivating people to embrace change is a tough order in any organization. In bureaucratic cultures, change is especially tough because the typically dysfunctional systems that run operations are so entrenched. System rigidity makes organizational barriers to successful change even tougher to over-come. Here are the barriers, along with the reason why the problems continue[1]:

1. **People aren't listened to (or perceive that they aren't).**

   Why does this non-productive behavior con-tinue? Because there aren't enough rewards/ motivation for leaders to change the way they manage.

2. **People from diverse levels and related groups within the organization aren't involved in planning changes.**
   Why? Leaders aren't aware of the huge benefits of wider participation and are afraid of the complications that including more people in the conversation may bring.

3. **People don't trust one another.**
   Why? Leaders don't sufficiently promote or give attention to open communication and sharing; i.e., transparency.

4. **People are afraid of failure**.
   Why? The penalties for failure are greater than the rewards for taking risk.

Good leaders will consistently and expeditiously accomplish their goals by removing impediments to proactive individual action. They will replace the impediments with positive tools for linking and developing people (described in previous chapters). By doing so, leaders neutralize the distractions and negative forces that work against effective change.

Removing the Barriers[2]
Recognizing these barriers, leaders can build an environment that openly embraces change. They can use every change project in every department and on every organizational issue as an opportunity to embed *inclusive* practices, using these steps:

1. **Effectively communicate the need for change to all stakeholders.**
   Provide enough information to ensure that people *believe* that a change must be made. Make the problems and needs very visible.

Provide examples of the problem, key statistics about what may happen without change; e.g., impact on productivity, profitability, and people. Provide visions of a more successful future for individuals and for the organization in a visible, understandable way.

2. **Listen to stakeholder concerns and needs.**
   Create an environment where the rewards for succeeding are great and the effects of failure are minimal, where people will voice their ideas and attempt improvements because they know their ideas have a good chance of being used to make a difference. Most people want to help, to show what they can do, to make a difference through their efforts.

   Conversely, when leaders do not openly solicit opinions about stakeholder concerns and needs, they send the message that they don't care about the employee/stakeholder or about *how* the goal or task is accomplished. They just want it done. Sending that message to stakeholders leads to an environment that invites shortcuts that affect quality, decisions that may jeopardize customer satisfaction, and worse, actions that skirt legal, moral and ethical boundaries.

3. **Communicate belief in the plan by using leaders whom stakeholders most respect — leaders from multiple levels and areas of the organization.**
   Place these peer leaders in visible positions — on key teams and as presenters in discussion sessions and staff meetings. Use their quotes and suggestions (with attribution) in newsletter clips about the project.

171

4. Involve stakeholders in a meaningful way.

- Build effective structure and processes for using the talents and knowledge of stakeholders. Infrastructure, as discussed in *Chapter 7 — Infrastructure,* enables those involved to take the initiative when needed to make the plan work. Satisfaction gained in doing tasks efficiently and successfully inspires people to do more. Good infrastructure enables that result to occur consistently and speedily.

- Ask for their opinions effectively, with an honest intention to learn more about the issue. People want to help. They know the difference between processes and surveys that are merely "window dressing" and sincere requests for their input.

- Facilitate people's ability to learn more about each other, not just about their tasks and duties, but also about their life learning and work experiences. Providing opportunities for individuals to share their diverse life skills and expertise contributes to organizational collaboration and to building intellectual capital.

- Publicly reinforce the value of people's contributions through use of a transparent approval process and speedy response. The death knell of sustainable, successful execution is struck when leaders seek input, involve people in developing solutions, and then ignore or stall action on the recommendations.

People Focus Rule #1:
Involvement Catches Opportunities
and Solves Problems Faster

Before starting an involvement process, leaders often ask, "But what if we decide we want to move in a different direction after involving a lot of people?" The solution to that potential problem is in the process itself.

If the process includes a strong assessment, good solution development, and an effective communication process (cross-organizational and multi-level), the need to do something else will arise during the change process itself, along with the plan for moving in the new direction.

The need to move in a new direction will happen through and with the people involved in the process instead of outside them.

The Pathway to Improvement — Part II

With this background in the importance of broad people involvement, using every type and size of change project to embed the practice of people involvement throughout the organization, let's now return to where we left off at the end of *Chapter 7 — Infrastructure.* We can continue with the final four steps that are needed to accomplish an effective Infrastructure improvement project (see *Appendix* for a summary).

These same steps are applicable for involving teams in accomplishing any change or new direction — for process improvement, strategic plan implementation, merger completion, organization restructuring, or new product/service roll-out. The objective of using teams to accomplish these final steps is to obtain the most knowledge while uniting the organization across diverse departments and levels.

We completed the first five steps (**Part I**) in *Chapter 7 — Infrastructure*:

*Phase One — **Assess** Current Situation*

1. Collect information about current status.

2. Summarize and analyze the issues (result: the Assessment Report).

3. Discuss and debate — inform and involve stakeholders.

*Phase Two — **Design** Solutions*

4. Collect information to develop alternatives.

5. Summarize and analyze information (result: the Design Report).

Step 5 ended with preparation to involve teams in further developing and implementing improvement solutions. Once the situation is thoroughly assessed, the alternatives are collected, and the major changes are determined, teams (comprised of individuals representing groups across the organization) can effectively perform the next steps.

Step 6. Develop Alternatives; Select Solutions and Strategies
By now, selected teams have had some exposure to both the Phase One Assessment Report and the Phase Two Design Report, either through direct participation or in group presentations. At their first meetings, the teams should review the areas assigned to them in order to gain greater understanding of the project's direction and goals. They

can then gather additional information as needed, discuss the pros and cons of possible alternatives, and, finally but successfully, develop the solutions and major recommendations to implement them.

An iterative process is key to successful results. The overall Three-Phase change process is iterative, with each step within each phase building on, affirming, or changing the previous step as additional knowledge is gained through exposure to new people and information. Step 6, in particular, is iterative as teams gather more information, assess alternatives and interact with other teams.

Team Management Guidelines
The process for managing teams is critical to effective project progress, using the structure and tools designed in Step 5, *Chapter 7 — Infrastructure.*

1. Link teams to enable them to each use the work of other teams and to avoid overlap. This can be done most effectively using a Steering Team, comprised of team chairs. They should meet regularly to:

    • Inform one another of their assigned areas and plans

    • Determine areas of overlap and negotiate responsibility

    • Resolve timeline inconsistencies

2. Once the Team Chairs thoroughly understand the change project and their responsibility areas, they can establish initial priority items and set/ revise the time deadlines. Change items should receive "A" priority if they:

- Are quick fixes that will give an immediate boost to the project ("low-hanging fruit")

- Are a major step toward achieving the goal

- Are most critical to accomplishing other changes, especially for other teams

People Focus Rule #2: Start Out Quick!

Start with recommendations for changes that can be implemented easily, will quickly reinforce the process, and will provide positive results of the change effort for all teams to see. Successful completion of even a simple solution motivates everyone to move forward with the more difficult ones and displays to all the process for completing recommendations.

3. Predetermine the process for reporting, discussion and approval of recommended changes; make the process very visible and use it consistently. Everyone involved needs to know that all teams and all initiatives will follow the same rules. All teams should know that if they follow the approval process, their recommendations will receive both respectful attention and much greater chance of being approved.

People Focus Rule #3: Build Trust

A consistent, credible approval process helps the organization build an environment of Trust.

4. The reporting and approval process should include the Process Guides in Step 5, **Box 7.6**:

   - Standard *process for developing the recommendation:* adequate research, detailed descriptions of alternatives and their pros and cons, "ball park" costs and resource needs for each alternative, and reasons for choosing the solution/change.

   - Standard *format for presentation* of the recommendation(s).

   - Standard *process for approval,* including preliminary review to assure that all steps are complete, that all questions raised by the Steering Team are answered, and that final approval by authorized person(s) is accomplished expeditiously.

   - Reasonable timelines for completion and implementation of recommendations

5. All teams need assurance that all other teams and individuals will perform assigned tasks on schedule. Major change projects, including infrastructure improvements and mergers, affect the entire organization; therefore, recommendation/change areas always (and should) overlap.

   Each team's work will impact the planning and implementation work of other teams. As a result, all teams should expect and be assured that all other teams conform to the established processes and timelines. The Accountability tools provided in Step 5, **Box 7.7** should be used zealously throughout Step 6 and subsequent implementation steps.

6. The Steering Group should assure that deadlines are met and that recommendations are adequately prepared. They should also assure that all teams will perceive the process as fair and consistent. When recommendations don't conform substantively to the requested approach and to the format guidelines, the Steering Group should return them to the assigned team with specific suggestions for improvement.

7. Leaders who established the new direction and macro timelines should approve team Recommendations and the revised timelines to assure consistency with the overall plan. Leaders must use the established Approval process to assure fairness and maintain the integrity of the change process. When improvement Recommendations substantively conform to the standard process, leaders should then carefully consider them and expedite the Approval process.

Leaders may think that it will take longer to get to implementation if *teams* are involved in efforts such as integrating software, revising personnel manuals, and developing sales materials. Quite the contrary. You can accomplish change organization-wide faster, more successfully and at less cost (time and $$) if you utilize stakeholder teams at every possible level.

For example, if one group, department, or division, appears to be seriously malfunctioning or is ineffective, the core problem is almost assuredly not just in that department or division. It is more likely that the department is in a critical position that makes the problem most visible there or the effect of the problem larger there. Finance Departments are a frequent example of this anomaly.

Phase Three – Execute Solutions

Implementation, too, should proceed in stages that involve many and diverse stakeholders to ensure quality and buy-in. As always, start with a process and structure and *document* both the process and the actual implementation plan. Clear processes and documents will make the implementation itself run more smoothly and enable monitoring and later improvements to be accomplished more efficiently.

Step 7. Research and Design Implementation Process and Structure.

A documented, detailed implementation plan will assure that you can firmly and consistently plant the solution throughout the organization. The plan should include a personnel structure, project timeline, benchmarks and measures of success, and an approval process.

Personnel Structure. The implementation structure should include:

- Representatives from affected segments of the organization on each implementation team

- Oversight, resource, and coordination group (Steering Group)

- Designated contact who has the knowledge and authority to approve plans

Timeline for Implementation steps, Benchmarks and Measures of Success. The Steering Group should focus on keeping timelines and teams on track. Timelines need to be realistic, but also consider that whether a group makes or slips its deadlines affects other steps and other groups, too. Develop project benchmarks to monitor progress.

179

Use Gantt or other tracking charts to show progress, with projected vs. actual dates for comparing and with summary overviews for use by leaders and other stakeholders who are not involved on project teams. Rather than just posting charts online, which requires purposeful time and attention, make progress on the project easily visible. Post the charts in workrooms, hallways and lounges so that everyone, even those not currently involved, can see the goals, dates and plans.

Tips to Build Involvement with Visibility and Communication

1. Discuss progress and accomplishment of benchmarks candidly in employee meetings. Point out as many involved performers as possible; give them credit for their accomplishments.

2. Hold employee dialogue and feedback sessions, including people on the teams and not. Acknowledge people's concerns, accept suggestions, and thank them publicly and specifically for their input.

3. Develop employee surveys of attitudes and concerns on the project and its progress. Publish results and sincerely thank contributors; openly and specifically thank those who developed and analyzed the survey results.

4. Send agendas for all team meetings in advance to signal the desire for meaningful participation in the meeting. Do meeting summaries immediately afterwards to affirm the contributions to progress and document assigned responsibilities for next steps.

5. Provide for team and organizational social events focused on celebrating change progress.

Box 8.1

180

In most organizations there is little preparation for group planning or decision-making. The resulting process is haphazard and inefficient; the result is frequently inconclusive. **Box 8.2** provides ideas that will speed the process and help to assure good results while building stronger internal teams.

Tips to Resolve Differences in Opinion Faster and Earlier

1. The better the Agenda, the more effective and the more efficient the meeting and resolution of issues. Think about the desired result in advance. Build the agenda to accomplish the result; stimulate thoughts in advance, when that is desired. When the issue is complex, plan to present information and preliminary discussion items that will lead to greater knowledge and common thinking about the situation in advance of the major discussion.

2. Coach leaders in effective *listening* and diagnostic *questioning* techniques. See **Diagnostic Interviewing for Consultants and Auditors – A Participative Approach to Problem Solving**, by John Quay.[3]

3. In brainstorming and problem-solving team activities on controversial issues, watch for and affirm **similarities** in thinking among groups whenever there is an opportunity to do so. With any group, there are always many more similarities in thinking and perception than the participants realize.

    When people see their similarities, they begin positive perceptions about one another that bring them together and enable them to reach common ground much more easily than when team leaders focus just on the differences of opinion. Additionally, once the similarities are visible and documented, the road to resolving differences and reaching agreement frequently develops.

Box 8.2

Effective implementation does take time, but it is more efficient to take the time up-front, with good planning, than it is to deal with the fallout, the missteps, and the problems that occur without it. With infrastructure especially, the best and most cost-effective time to build and to improve is *ahead* of growth. That way, all parts function effectively, in sync, as needed.

Good infrastructure, including effective communication systems and processes, provides for people focus. Good infrastructure enables greater creativity, fosters trust in leaders and in each other, and therefore will lead to increased organization strength and competitive advantage. That is just what happened when *Silent Spring* used the change steps outlined above and in *Chapter 7* to improve its infrastructure.

Silent Spring, Part 2

The Solution: *Silent Spring was determined to fix its organizational problems. An outside coordinator/ consultant, along with an ad hoc internal team of selected Directors, interviewed all eighteen Directors.*

After analyzing interviews and collected reports, charts, etc., the coordinator and the inside team targeted preliminary areas for improvement. Outside specialists were brought in to assess and develop solutions in key infrastructure problem areas within Purchasing, Information Technology, and Human Resource departments. Representatives from various departments and levels filled predetermined teams to brainstorm strategies for change and to assure effective implementation.

Major changes were accomplished for the organization structure itself. The objective was to improve accountability and collaboration:

1. *A formal Executive Team was established to coordinate activities and advise the CEO. The eighteen previously independent departments were linked through a more formal structure that highlighted overlapping roles and common interests.*

2. *All Departments were re-evaluated: some were terminated, some were expanded, and others were reconfigured. A Personnel Department was established. The new Human Resources manager, along with a Human Resources consulting firm, put solid policies, systems, and processes into place.*

3. *The new Financial Assets and Information Services Department hired a systems specialist to obtain and implement adequate financial and information reporting systems for the benefit of employees and key outside stakeholders.*

4. *The new Purchasing Department combined purchasing activities from all departments and programs in one place. This change enabled volume purchases and establishment of good purchasing practices and controls. The resulting savings were used to hire an experienced Purchasing Manager, who significantly* **cut operating and administrative supply** *costs while increasing the quality of purchased products and services. Morale increased with the reduced workload (and headaches!) in every department.*

5. *All dining operations were combined under the supervision of one highly qualified manager; the quality and consistency of dining services*

> *throughout the organization greatly improved. Centrally located food production replaced silo food preparation operations within each division. Employees, students, and visitors were ecstatic about the major improvement in food quality.*

The Result: *Once people no longer had to perform tasks for which they had little training or skill, and high-quality professionals — rather than managers with little expertise — were efficiently running former problem areas from central locations, the Silent Spring working environment improved dramatically. Communication across departments soared. Errors caused by inconsistent or non-existent policies and processes decreased and so did everyone's level of frustration. Creativity and growth occurred even in the departments with the worst performance.*

At a macro level, Silent Spring's Capital Campaign was hugely successful, too. Its growth rate and market share, ability to attract and retain the best employees, and capacity all increased. Overall, Silent Spring developed a stronger, better working environment that also attracted and enabled better leaders. The critical component that permitted these improvements was the major change from a woefully inadequate infrastructure to a solid foundation.

Step 8. Summarize Implementation; Develop Tools
Silent Spring's major infrastructure improvements financed its growth initiatives. Future stability was ensured through increased productivity and significantly improved morale and internal creativity.

These amazing results were due partly to the iterative process used to assess, develop/design, and implement the new infrastructure. This iterative, phased change process — at *Silent Spring* and elsewhere — creates greater stakeholder under-standing, breaks down silos, and enables broad levels of collaboration. The iterative change process also embeds people-focused, team-based change concepts within the DNA of the organization.

Once the initial need for change is identified by leaders, all the next steps should be developed and documented by teams. With each step, the teams take on more ownership for the change/improve-ment effort. And, by *Steps 8 and 9*, the teams have the knowledge and collaborative ability to accom-plish steps efficiently and effectively (see *Appendix* for a summary). The organizational wisdom has increased.

People Focus Rule #4:
Recognize the Iterative Process for Its
Value — Building Organization Wisdom
and Better Internal Decisions

Many problems, especially infrastructure ones, are invisible until teams and leaders start analyzing the situation, designing the solution, and implementing changes. Some subprocesses, reports, and experiences surface only as implementation begins.

Recognizing in advance that the process will be iterative prepares the teams to see issues when they surface and then move to improve them as part of the process, rather than as a distraction. The major benefit, in addition to a more successful project result, is the many previously invisible problems that are solved in the process, as well as the increased skills of team members in seeing and immediately solving potential impediments to successful implementation.

Step 9. Implement, Monitor, and Improve

Once the implementation plan is documented, it is ready to roll out. Develop presentation materials and the dissemination approach in advance to assure effective communication and understanding.

Present the implementation plan to small groups rather than large audiences. Presentations should include prepared questions that invite interaction and suggestions from the groups. These interactive small-group discussions set the stage for future suggestions from departments and individuals as they implement the changes.

Post-Implementation Reassessment

Is the change effective? A critical final step is to review the original objective, along with the project accomplishments, steps still to be completed, new issues that have arisen during the change/improvement process, and the process for resolving them. Schedule this step for soon after implementation is complete to keep the project on track and assure that unforeseen related issues don't grow to negate its benefits.

As the organization gains experience in making changes using a thoughtful, inclusive, and iterative process, the steps become embedded and therefore simpler and faster each time they are used. Making changes, both effectively and efficiently, becomes second nature to stakeholders at all levels and in all areas of the organization. The environment then becomes one that welcomes and thrives on change rather than fearing it.

Continual Reassessment of Infrastructure

Good infrastructure is both a constant improvement project and a requirement for healthy growth and sustainability. People can't function effectively, in any department, without strong infrastructure. So, infrastructure needs to be regularly assessed. A key leader, preferably someone at a Director or VP level, should be assigned to assure infrastructure strength and compatibility with the organization as it grows and changes. **Box 8.3** provides a starting point for an assessment process.

Questions for
Evaluating Organizational Infrastructure

1. Is the organization's reporting/responsibility structure effective or does the structure inhibit effective change and growth towards its Vision?

2. Do internal communication processes and tools help or hinder the smooth flow of information?

3. Do internal reports provide the greatest and most valuable information efficiently, in ways that foster good decision-making?

4. Do electronic systems link information and a variety of user departments and organizational levels effectively and efficiently?

5. Are those responsible for developing and assessing these factors evaluated on their improvement?

6. Is effective performance in these infrastructure areas visible to all stakeholders at the same importance level as sales, operations, and financial performance indicators?

Box 8.3

If performance in these infrastructure areas is not visible or valued, IT IS IMPOSSIBLE for other areas of the organization to function at optimum levels. Think of the strongest, most resilient species in nature — ants. Without an established infrastructure and linked connection to all in it, the entire colony dies a slow, painful death. When the infrastructure doesn't work, the colony goes. That's what's happening to my once-favorite airline.

Planet Earth Airlines

I worked until 2 AM and, in my stupor, set my alarm for 4 PM instead of 4 AM. I realized what I had done as soon as I got up, too late to make my 7 AM cross-country flight. I immediately called Planet Earth to reschedule and was told they had nothing left that could get me there by the next morning. Pushed, the reservations agent finally found a seat for me and, because of my almost 1M lifetime miles with the airline, grabbed it. She said I didn't need to go to the airport early as a standby since I had a confirmed seat; I could just go to a ticket counter at 3:00 PM.

When I arrived at the ticket counter, there was no new reservation in my name — and all flights were full. Nor was there any record in the system of my phone conversation with the reservations agent. My entire flight itinerary had been canceled and noted "no show." Not only that: I'd been given bad instructions when I made the new reservation. A supervisor said that if I had gone to the airport when I woke up, I would have been put on an earlier flight because of my many miles with the airline. The supervisor who explained this apologized profusely and then said this was the third time that day a mistake like this had been made.

"Will you report this so the company can fix the process and problem?" I asked.

"No. They will just write me off as a 'disgruntled desk agent.' It won't do any good and it will hurt me to say anything."

I've been flying with this airline for thirty years and want to be loyal; but I won't be flying with them again. It's not worth it. I know many others who have made the same decision for the same reasons: frustration, stressful conversations that go nowhere and, most of all, large amounts of wasted time. Employees have insufficient knowledge and access to company information, are afraid to talk to their managers, and are not empowered to take action on behalf of customers. The company keeps lowering prices, but they are losing customers — and managers will probably never know why.

The *Planet Earth Airlines* situation is typical of the kind of intersecting problems that work against resilience:

- the processes are dysfunctional

- the environment does not empower employees to report and solve problems

- the culture diminishes employee trust in management

The above problems combine to create a downward spiral most companies can't stop unless they turn all three around simultaneously, something that is very difficult to do. Sadly, this triple threat strikes the death knell for many organizations with great products — like my once-favorite airline.

It takes a great and selfless leader to change systemic, embedded negative issues and to build environments that support individual initiative and collaboration. A selfless leader is needed to build infrastructure that supports effective individual and organizational performance.

It is difficult to motivate people to go the extra mile to accomplish their day-to-day tasks while also working on change initiatives. It is hard and often leads to resentment unless people truly believe that the organization has the ability and the will/desire to accomplish the effort.

Only an obviously selfless leader has the power to convince all stakeholders of the organization's ability and to enable the trust that leads them to have a real desire to help. It is tough to build *faith* in the organization *before* the new environment exists — only this sincerely selfless leader can do that.

PART 3 – UNITY

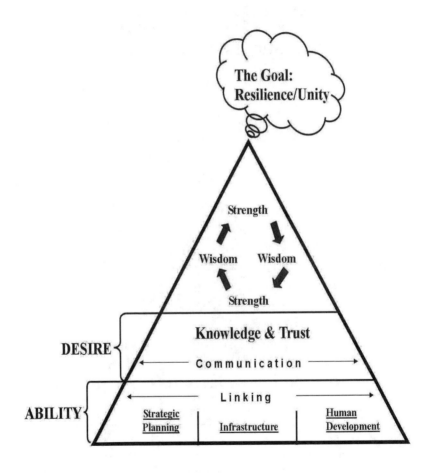

Chapter 9:
Selflessness
Achieving Successful Results as One

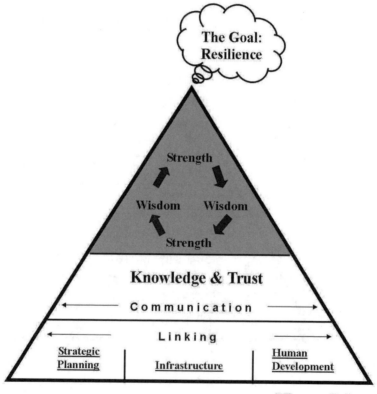

Figure 9.1

P&T

A big international CPA firm, P&T, decided to make major changes in Madison, its worst-performing location in the U.S. They brought in a new managing partner for the office, Don Huston. They also decided to acquire Silver and Goldman (S&G), a local CPA firm, which had grown in ten years from one person to the largest local firm in the city. S&G had a reputation for high-quality work and was very profitable. Huston gave S&G's founder and managing partner, Travis Goldman, a mission: "Help build P&T's Madison office as you did S&G."

The Governor asked P&T, with Travis Goldman as its representative, to join his upcoming trade mission to Japan, along with leaders from thirty of Madison's major manufacturers. The Governor also asked P&T to provide Travis's business development advisory services to the thirty firm leaders while on the trip and international trade coaching using P&T's experts in Madison and Japan. Participation in the trade mission was an opportunity for P&T to play a starring role with those leading manufacturers and also with the state's increasingly important trade activities with Japan.

While each manufacturing company paid a fee of $30,000 to help cover trade mission costs, P&T was asked to cover only Travis' direct travel. Incredibly, Don said "No," unless Travis guaranteed the $4,000 would be covered by fees from new manufacturing clients in the same fiscal quarter. Because of timing and process for client development, that condition was impossible to fulfill and Travis had to say so.

The trip would have given P&T and their international specialists an opportunity to gain sustained, high-quality visibility with some of Madison's most prominent companies at a time when they and Don, as a new managing partner, needed a major boost.

But Don said no because he did not want Travis, as a new partner from a local firm, to be the firm's representative on this important state project. Don was more concerned with bolstering his own new position than about the growth of the firm.

The result was that P&T lost not only a significant chance to grow in the current year and even more in the future, but also the high performance "rainmaker."

The moral from the P&T/S&G story is that the attitude of leaders can kill or stunt even the most assured growth plans.

There is only one way to be a successful leader: care more about the Vision and the people you lead than about your own comfort and desires. Only a small percentage of leaders, in my experience, can do that. But that requirement separates real leaders from the simply charismatic or "wannabe" ones.

Real leaders put their own egos and preferences aside to focus on the long-term development of the organization. It takes automatic self-talk that says, "I don't care if this may hurt or not benefit me. I want to make it happen so that the people and the organization can succeed in this effort." The result is frequently incredible success, which invariably reflects on the leader.

When people perceive that their leader thinks first about him- or herself, they become suspicious of all actions by the leader, whether actually driven by self-interest or not. They don't trust the leader, and without trust, people don't take risks, they don't do hard jobs willingly, and they frequently don't act when perhaps they should.

Suspicion about leader intention almost always reduces the level of communication within organizations. When people perceive that their leaders use information for their own personal benefit, they withhold potentially valuable communication that might help to achieve goals or solve problems.

Teach Selflessness

Good to Great[1] leaders are selfless. They lead with *Emotional Intelligence*[2,3], as Dr. Daniel Goleman's groundbreaking research proved. They value and build an environment of *Absolute Honesty*[4] as Larry Johnson and Bob Phillips detailed. They lead with moral courage and integrity. They are like the risk-takers in *Those Who Dare*[5], Katherine Martin's book about people who saw unfair situations and faced possibly damaging results for themselves but took on the challenge anyway. They displayed high-level personal strength and wisdom — the hallmark of great leaders.

Great goals will be achieved only with a truly self-less leader. There are many examples. The amazing Oregon Ducks football team of 2009-2012 finished their four-year, winningest period in team history. They won three conference titles, went to four BCS Bowl games and, in January, 2013, won their second BCS victory in a row against Kansas State in the Fiesta Bowl. The Ducks did it under one man who became head coach in 2009. At the start of the fourth season, an announcer at the Oregon-Arkansas State game noted, "The best thing about this [Oregon] team is their unselfishness."

It's the same thing Brian Doyle wrote about the national title-winning women's soccer team at the University of Portland — their amazing generosity.[6]

You can develop a great strategic plan, improve the systems, ensure that good processes and communication mechanisms are in place. You can work to accomplish an environment that builds trust, motivation and confidence in stakeholders, which leads to unselfishness. Selfless leaders are synthesizers who link pieces effectively to create the DNA of a resilient organization — they are the catalysts for change. Once Resilience DNA is established and embedded by a selfless leader, the organization can survive bad leaders and even good leaders who fall.

Teams that apparently come out of nowhere to become consistent winners are usually known for the selflessness of their individual team members. As every good parent knows, the most effective way to teach any concept is to demonstrate it. Becoming *visibly* selfless requires self-discipline and self-awareness, especially with today's environment of ultra-consumerism and self-indulgence. It takes being in touch with one's higher self — the font of wisdom and strength.

One of many good Great Recession outcomes is that a large percentage of the world came to realize that material goods, in an increasingly greater amount, are not everything. We learned that we can be happy with much less, but it takes a change of heart — and spirit — to consistently reside in that place despite increased success.

Being a successful boss, consultant, coach or any kind of leader demands the same talent as being a good teacher. It requires the ability to reach each team or person, influence and inspire them, and then enable them to do their best by providing them with the best tangible and intangible tools. The most effective way to teach selflessness is to lead by example, focusing on five areas:

1. **Respect** Your Team
2. Take Personal Risks – Have **Courage**
3. **Participate** *with* Your Team
4. Practice **Humility**
5. Guard Your **Integrity**

1. R- E- S- P- E- C- T . . . Your Team

Do everything possible to help build people's self-esteem. Sometimes that means not taking credit where due and not being quick to blame, even when it might be merited. Think about the kindly priest in *Les Miserables*, who turned around the hero's life by not publicly blaming him for his theft of church silver. Here are some ways to practice that respectful behavior that builds people up in the workplace:

- Even if only 10% of a problem is likely yours, be first to take responsibility for it. You want people working on a project to feel positive about their progress, not focus on their minor missteps. Usually, people know they goofed and feel guilty. You don't want them to dwell on mistakes on the way to accomplishment.

> **Selfless Leader Rule #1:**
> **Guilt and failure feelings slow progress.**
> **Take action to minimize negative**
> **emotions.**

- Psychologists agree that people, at least in western cultures, tend to take 10 times more offense than is given. People usually don't intend to insult or injure us. Our own negative biases and insecurity lead us to interpret it that way.

  You can't effectively watch or listen to gain new information while trying to analyze a comment or situation for possible negative effects on you. Instead, immediately force yourself to think of one or two positive interpretations. Then, focus on *listening* and *watching* from that positive perspective.

Selfless Leader Rule #2:
Give everyone the benefit of the doubt.
That mental attitude will help you to
listen better and learn more.

- Respect people's right to privacy, to tell their story about what happened to them in a perceived negative situation in *their* way. Never talk about others disparagingly or share their flaws unless absolutely necessary and then only in a professional manner and out of sight and earshot of other employees.

  For a leader, there is frequently a grey area between responsible communication and destructive talk and actions. It's all about balance; that grey line about the right thing to do is often hazy. How does a leader decide? Think about the Golden Rule and pray for guidance to do or say the right thing.

Selfless Leader Rule #3:
The Golden Rule: Do unto others as you
would have them do unto you.

2. Take Personal Risks – Have Courage

It's hard. It's scary sometimes. Keep reminding yourself, whenever you think, "They might think negatively about me," or "This might happen to me," that the only way to move forward successfully is to act in the best interests of your organization and its people. Thinking about what might happen to you and then acting defensively to avoid any possibility is the surest way to failure.

Newcastle Arts and Culture Society

Trish Alexander became the new Executive Director of the Newcastle Arts and Culture Society following Ellen Mapleton's retirement after 24 years in that position. Under Ellen's leadership, the sleepy local society soared to new heights. Nationally regarded, it was also a prominent regional force with business and governmental communities. Ellen's legacy intimidated Trish; she was overwhelmed by everyone's expectations that she successfully accomplish their ambitious plans for building a major new center for the Society.

Trish was afraid of negative comparison of her more laid-back, softer style with Ellen's commanding presence, especially after experiencing several Board meetings that didn't go as well as she planned. So Trish decreased the number of Board meetings from monthly to quarterly, decreased their length and content, and reduced reports to the Board. Rather than risk similar difficult meetings, Trish decided not to convene any meetings of the recently formed Friends of Newcastle Arts and Culture, which Ellen had created to help support the Society's growth and development plans.

Because Trish also feared the staff's comparison of her with their beloved predecessor Director, she avoided involving them in her decision-making and planning activities. She rarely held staff meetings and increasingly managed by one-on-one directives that were frequently inconsistent and contradictory. Staff resigned and contributions fell. Construction stopped for lack of funds; future plans were shelved. Board members resigned and were not replaced. When individual Society friends offered to step in as interim staff or to help restart planning and activities, they were rebuffed or ignored. The Newcastle Arts and Culture Society was on a downward spiral.

Newcastle is a dramatic, but not that unusual, example. Fear of failure, by both executives and external consultants, diminishes the possibility for many organizations to make major advances and to achieve stellar growth, especially for those with outside "evaluators" (e.g., Boards, voters, stockholders, funders). Both internal and external consultants frequently take the "safe route" in their reports to management because that's what their clients want to hear: recommendations based on the current situation and most likely, near-term effects because short-range plans are more certain of success. The organization's purported strategic plan is anything but.[7]

Too many leaders try to play it safe. CEOs and other key leaders hold back their full endorsement and visible leadership waiting for a consensus or mandate. They don't want to risk coming out too strong on a particular initiative or new direction until they see overwhelming support from their constituents. But in order to fully commit, stakeholders need first to see the passionate commitment of their leaders to a strong solution or new direction. Instead, in an effort to make everyone happy, many leaders dilute the strategy so much that it cannot effectively accomplish the desired change.

Leaders today are frequently paralyzed by fear; they are so afraid of making mistakes and of criticism from their "evaluators" that they condemn themselves and their organizations to failure or to only short-term, mediocre accomplishment.

Today, in this atmosphere of fear of reprisals and of short-term, safe decisions, selfless leaders must use their analytical skills and organizational knowledge to first provide transparent, solidly accurate information as early as possible, then assure collaboration in assessing alternatives, and finally, lead decision-making and effective implementation for the long-term, greater benefit of their organizations and its stakeholders.

The word that best describes those who built and assured America's success in becoming the world's most powerful nation is *Audacity*. They **dared**. Those past leaders also worked hard, alongside one another, and believed and trusted in God's help. To be successful, you can't be afraid to take risks; you can't be afraid to fail. Henry Ford didn't see his failures as such; he called them "setbacks" and forged ahead.

3. Participate *with* Your Team

Upper-level leaders are the primary link in unifying the organization; they provide the big-picture links with outside resources and across the organization to the internal directors and managers. Managers and directors are the interpreter leaders to all stakeholders: customers, mainstream production, and other internal resources. See *Chapter 2 — Chemistry 101, Figure 2.2.*

Leaders at any level can successfully facilitate change only if they truly *understand* their troops. CEOs who react to problems without deeply involving their stakeholders frequently create even greater problems. Truly sustainable solutions are built only by substantively weaving the underlying processes and people development into them.

Self-less leaders learn enough about their stakeholders to answer these questions before moving forward with any initiative:

1. What are their individual needs?

2. How do their needs affect their jobs?

3. How can they be involved with the transition and with the future after the change?

4. What do they most need to know in order to prepare for the transition and for the future?

Awareness of stakeholders' needs and focus on providing a *comprehensive* solution gives superior results:

- Shortens the time it takes to successfully implement

- Assures more successful results

- Reduces the possibility of future errors and problems

- Creates more accurate solutions

- Minimizes customer frustrations in the transition

The most successful leaders in developing and changing their organizations work constantly at understanding and involving all their stakeholders.

Henry Ford had his flaws as a people manager, but he was amazingly participatory on the production floor. He was visible there; he watched and regularly jumped in to help when a problem or need arose. His people loved him; they knew he cared about them. When there was a new goal to increase production or to change processes, they worked zealously and overtime on their own because they saw his dream and believed in him. As a result, Ford Motor Co. accomplished incredible feats and achieved amazing growth.

Bobby Beathard[8,9], called "The Smartest Man in Football" by *Sports Illustrated,* was the General Manager of the Washington Redskins and, later, of the San Diego Chargers. During his tenure, he led teams to the Super Bowl five times. Bobby's job was to recruit, hire (and fire) players and coaches. He did many things differently from other GMs, but he was especially known for two things: working out potential players himself and going after people who had raw talent and good character rather than flash and renown.

Bobby didn't just do his job with research and with phone calls from his headquarters office. He sleuthed and visited in places other GMs didn't go; he stayed in good shape so that he could run potential hires through plays himself — see their reactions and how they learned. He talked to them and their coaches, quizzed them, and learned about their values and how they thought. His players and coaches loved him for his involvement with them — before and after they were hired.

And, of course, there is **Chip Kelly**, so successful that after his fourth season as head coach of the University of Oregon's football team, he was recruited for the position of head coach by no less than four pro NFL teams. Chip lived and breathed with his team; he was one of them and they loved him. He preached that they could win anything if they just focused on "winning the day" at every opportunity, and his troops believed him. They were successful, every year, from the year he started.[10]

4. Practice Humility
As great philosophers such as Confucius ("Humility is the solid foundation of all the virtues") and Socrates noted, nothing truly great can be accomplished without humility. Our egos prevent us from

taking steps that would result in major improvements and also to accelerated development in every endeavor. Our egos lead us to make mistakes that we later regret, in both public and private arenas.

Arrogance (i.e., self-important thinking) damages forward movement. Over and over again, arrogance, which is the opposite of humility, hurts us. We all see that result in ourselves, in the most powerful companies, and in many sports teams. Many saw it happen to the apparently invincible University of Oregon Ducks in 2011. They hadn't lost a game. After they demolished #3 in the country Stanford, 53-30, at Stanford, the press talked about Oregon's star player as the next Heisman Trophy winner and predicted that Coach Kelly would go on to become an NFL coach. The following week the Ducks lost at home, humiliatingly, to #18-ranked USC. It was Chip Kelly's first home loss in his tenure as head coach. The Ducks dropped from their #4 position and lost their chance to try for the national BCS championship again.

That situation happens in business a lot. The mighty at the top fall to much humbler competitors. It is tough for people who have proven success and acclaim not to be affected by that acclaim. It takes constant awareness of the potential dangers of being overly confident. Chip Kelly warned about it all the time; the seemingly invincible Oregon Ducks still fell. For good leaders, avoiding arrogance in the face of success requires self-discipline: to act with the knowledge that true strength does not lie in promoting and advancing ourselves but in building the strength of others — the workers and other stakeholders around us.

Being a good leader is all about balance. This means providing strong direction while also giving selfless assistance. It means being a servant leader to all stakeholders. Along the road to building self-awareness, there are two ego-controlling rules to remember and to practice:

- Don't be afraid of not looking good.

- Don't think about what you could accomplish or what you would do if you were the one in the limelight.

Self-less Leader Rule #4:
Watch for Opportunities to Praise

Look for ways to build up your people. Acknowledge your people's special gifts at every opportunity with words like: "Wow! You came up with that idea?! It was a powerful one!" and "You worked there? No wonder you are so good at sales!" and "Your Dad was a carpenter? No wonder you are so creative. It's in your genes!"

Make these comments in front of others, whenever possible. Especially watch for opportunities to build up someone who is being widely maligned for a negative trait. Building up public awareness of a person's positive traits strengthens him/her to overcome negative traits.

In little ways, too, you can build your own ego control and avoid tendencies that lead to arrogance. At the same time, you can significantly build the trust of those around you by saying two things as frequently as appropriate:

- "I don't know." Say that whenever you can instead of thinking that you need to have an answer for everyone. Otherwise, the result is that you bluff and hedge with answers that aren't meaningful and everyone will know it.

- "I goofed." Say it even when only a portion of the goof was yours. Others will know that there was fault in many places, not just with you. They will respect you for taking responsibility. Hopefully, others will emulate your approach and help to build a culture of selflessness within the organization.

Here are some great words from great thinkers. Reflect on them when your negative self argues against the "I don't know," "I goofed" response.

"I have three precious things which I hold and prize. The first is gentleness; the second is frugality; the third is humility, which keeps me from putting myself before others. Be gentle and you can be bold: be frugal and you can be liberal; avoid putting yourself before others and you can become a leader among men." **Lao Tzu**

"There is nothing noble in being superior to your fellow man; true nobility is being superior to your former self." **Ernest Hemingway**

"A great man is always willing to be little." **Ralph Waldo Emerson**

"True humility is not thinking less of yourself; it is thinking of yourself less." **C.S. Lewis**

5. Guard and Maintain Your Integrity
Integrity is defined most commonly as "honesty, sincerity and transparency, consistency and wholeness of actions and methods." In ethics, humility is usually defined as honesty and truthfulness in the motivations for one's actions. Integrity is the exact opposite of hypocrisy. The lack of leader integrity

destroys an organization's capability to achieve successful, sustainable results. *Dahlstrom Inner City League,* introduced in *Chapter 2 — Chemistry 101,* experienced that result as they worked to achieve their major growth goals.

Dahlstrom Inner City League, Part 2

In an attempt to turn around the downward spiral, Board members and other Dahlstrom stakeholders developed a very exciting Vision for the future. They designed strategies for improving visibility and for expanding programs.

Charlie Hampson, the founder/program director and Board Chair, was not willing to publicly challenge some of the new directions and activities that came out of the group planning sessions, even though he disagreed with them. Rather than voice objections in the meetings, where the group could confront and debate his alternative views, he remained silent. The group interpreted his silence as consent, as agreement with the new plans.

After the planning sessions, as Board Chair and Program Director, Charlie changed the Plan. He moved to develop and implement a different direction on his own with key internal staff. He ignored the planning session work of key stakeholders and did not share his intentions to move in a different direction. He didn't want to deal with conflict in the group sessions or appear to be a "wet blanket" dampening the excitement and enthusiasm of the change-focused planning group. He figured that he would roll out his own exciting plan when it was ready and gain stakeholder support then.

The group later realized that Charlie didn't value their efforts and opinions. His dishonest and opaque actions damaged their trust in him. Disillusioned, they lost faith in the future plan, in Charlie, and in

207

the organization. They became lukewarm, rather than committed, participants and leaders. When issues arose that they might otherwise champion or take the initiative to resolve, they were disinterested bystanders at best. Charlie lost positive forces and allies because of his desire to protect himself, to avoid confrontation, and to assure that the plan would be done his way.

This sad result occurs very frequently, perhaps not as dramatically and as visibly, but always causes negative, backward reactions that severely damage the organization's forward movement and resilience. The negative reactions could always have been avoided by a leader who acted with honesty, transparency, and integrity.

Selflessness Rule #5:
Guard Your Own Integrity First

The key to guarding integrity is to constantly watch your reactions:

1. Do what you say.

2. Say what you will do.

3. Do what you believe.

Acting with integrity is frequently uncomfortable and scary. But the result is always far more positive for both the person and the organization than taking the perceived easier, more self-protective route.

The Final Self-less Leader's Step: Teach Unity

People know when a leader is acting out of his or her own self-interest rather than for the good of the organization. A self-sacrificing attitude builds resilient, sustainably winning organizations, from ant kingdoms to the Lady Pilots at the University of Portland to Nike's founders, Phil Knight and Bill Bowerman. The leaders in these organizations all cared more about the organization than about themselves. They were successful because of that goal-focused, self-less attitude. Developing that attitude is the challenge and the test for all leaders.

It takes personal strength and wisdom to be a self-less, successful leader. To successfully build a resilient organization, you have to be willing to take a lot of arrows along the way. You have to view yourself as an instrument to enable achievement of a higher purpose. The reward for exercising those highest-level personal traits is that, from the fruits they bear, everyone in the organization will be empowered and enabled to grow in strength and wisdom.

Chapter 10:
The Resilient Organization
Attaining the Ultimate Goal by
Acting with a Collective Heartbeat

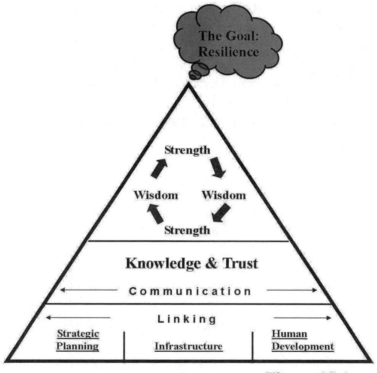

Figure 10.1

" . . . the coolest thing of all about the 2005 Pilot women's soccer team wasn't [that they won their second U.S. national college soccer title in four years]. It was the way they played, the verve and dash and zest and humor and camaraderie and creativity and coherence and generosity and quicksilver flow of their game as they bent it to their remarkable wills, the astounding instantaneous passes, the liquid geometry, the relentless energy, the constant laughter, the eerie calm, the heartfelt and hilarious bond with their fellow students, the patient sinuous ferocity of their play.

It was the way they were serious students still even as they became ever more obviously the best team in America. It was the way they were part of the crowd and not at all sneeringly above it as with so many athletes. It was the way they ran together in a ragged laughing line into the student section applauding and embracing their classmates. It was the way they ran together to the public grandstand applauding their fans. It was the way they ranged along the railings after games and signed autographs and shook hands and chaffed children for as long as there was a child awed and agog. It was the way they became the cheerful stitches binding a whole new fabric of community, far larger and more joyous and more appreciative of shared joy than ever before . . ."

Extract from *"The Joy,"* by Brian Doyle[1]

The principles presented in this book are essential to successful major change and for dynamic growth. They are vital to move towards the most desirable phase of organizational development: *acting with a collective heartbeat,* as ONE. As the Lady Pilots soccer team showed year after year, even after facing the untimely death of their beloved coach, unified organizations are more successful at changing than siloed ones.

That's why underdog teams in sports or in business, like FedEx, Avis and Nike, so often come from behind and slay giants: The greater and more visionary the goal, the tougher the challenge, the more overwhelming the odds, the greater the potential for incredible unity. When the shared vision is clear and the *esprit de corps* is high, the chances of winning increase. The chances increase because with a shared vision and high morale, everyone knows what to do and how doing it contributes to achieving the common goal.

That's why new organizations, those with an inspired and inspiring entrepreneur and without vast resources, can grow so quickly and so well. The linkages among team members are strong because the group is small; everyone can literally touch everyone else. Communication is open and constant; everyone has immediate access to the latest issues, needs, problems and developments. Every person knows everyone else's strengths so well that they can call on the right people whenever they need them. Instantaneous adaptability of tasks and responses becomes routine. The concepts that enable rapid implementation (optimum involvement and empowerment of people) work naturally and effectively in small, start-up organizations.

Larger, more mature organizations have more trouble mobilizing their troops and overcoming differences when facing new directions and conflicting alternatives, even those that pride themselves on being collaborative and team-oriented. They just can't achieve the unity that enabled them to take on giants and to scale mountains as easily (or with the same joy) as they did when they were growing.

Unity dissipates quickly as an organization grows and the focus is more on building new product sectors and setting up departments. The importance of maintaining unity and core passion is forgotten in the scramble to build greater capacity.

Organizations that have lost unity and passion can always regain them and those who never had them can acquire them by building the three components that comprise *Ability*:

- *Visionary*, unifying strategic plans

- *Effective* infrastructures that focus on individual growth

- Environments that support the growth of *trust*, motivation and confidence in all stakeholders

With each step that is taken to build and embed strength in these centralizing and passion-building components, organizations are able to accomplish a healthier organizational DNA — a DNA that will survive attacks by both mutant internal cells and external viruses. As a result, the organization gains and sustains the capability to *act with a collective heartbeat:* Resilience.

Sustainable Success Rule #1

Sustainable success is not achieved with good change *management*. It is *Resilience* — the fuel of adaptability — that enables sustained success.

213

Maintaining Strength

There are myriad reasons why unity dissipates as organizations grow. Even positive attributes and tools require mindful, big-picture awareness and review as the organization changes, lest they morph into negative detractors, undesirable traits that will inhibit successful change.

For example, purposefully designed organization structure and well-documented processes provide infrastructure for successful change in a growing, increasingly complex organization. When leaders consistently use the well-documented, visible infrastructure to make decisions and manage their organizations, people take risks. They *trust* that if they take the established route and are diligent, their plans will have a good chance of success. But when leaders too rigidly enforce the established infrastructure, without displaying good judgment and common sense in applying it, established infrastructure will have the opposite effect: It smothers creativity and agility. See *Chapter 5 — Process Power* and *Chapter 7 — Infrastructure*.

Effective infrastructure, including transparent methods for modifying it, aids in developing and empowering people and therefore leads to greater resilience. Mindful focus on the following six key environmental attributes and tools, all working together, enables good leaders to build and sustain resilience:

1. Honesty and integrity must be fostered and rewarded within the organization to build an environment of trust and collaboration.

   The CPA profession should be the epitome of this virtue. CPAs take an oath to protect the public when receiving their licenses to practice their important service. CPAs swear to act in the public interest, not their own, in circumstances that may put them at odds with less-scrupulous clients or less-honest supervisors at their firms. Commitment to this state-mandated role is a condition of retaining CPAs' exclusive license to perform financial assurance services.

Learning and practicing that "protection of the public" role well gives most CPAs an internal attitude of selflessness. When CPAs forget their primary role, as some have done very publicly, bad audits result. The CPAs went along with client desires. They justified doing so, even when client desire conflicted with the best interests of the third-party, financial statement user, because the client pays the bill. Some CPA firms have enabled this distorted thinking by their inordinate focus on profits and growth rather than on their central purpose of providing an appropriate opinion on the fairness of the financial statements for the public's protection.

Absolute honesty and integrity should be non-negotiable in all organizations. As CPA firms and many other entities have very publicly demonstrated in the wake of the Enron implosion, inattention to this virtue will most certainly have disastrous effects for organizations.[2, 3]

Disastrous effects aside, if a culture of honesty and integrity is not promoted, trust will not grow within the organization. And without trust, a resilient DNA is not possible.

2. Good communication systems and processes facilitate openness and sharing. They enable transparent actions and free access to both

information and people, as needed, for every stakeholder within the organization.

Good communication systems and processes also promote the spread of good values, increased knowledge and trust. This enables constant learning and improvement in the direction that benefits both the organization and each individual within it.

3. Understanding is the capability to internalize and to process knowledge at a deep mental and spiritual level. Understanding enables effective application of knowledge. Understanding adds awareness of the effects of facts — about events, reactions, relationships — on people and on systems (mechanical and human).

Developed skills in both listening and asking questions help to build understanding, which thereby strengthens a positive and constant learning environment.

Diagnostic interviewing[4] is critical for any professional whose job it is to learn important information from people — CPAs, lawyers, psychologists, human resource professionals, diplomats. Use of the diagnostic interviewing method enables the interviewer to gain true understanding rather than what the person interviewed wants the questioner to believe.

Diagnostic interviewing techniques can help any leader to be a more effective listener. Using the techniques will help good leaders to understand the needs, issues and concerns of stakeholders.

The Socratic method of dialogue utilizes questions rather than rhetoric to prompt listeners to consider alternative approaches.[5] It

216

is such an effective method of helping people to learn other perspectives that Socrates was executed for inciting rebellion, not by promoting his views but by asking questions! People learn most, at a deeper level, when they are prompted to think for themselves, not when they are directed to think in a certain way.

4. *Meaningful* involvement creates a positive environment of inclusivity rather than exclusivity. When people believe that they are part of the process rather than slaves to it, they want to help make the effort a success. This change in attitude builds an organization-wide desire and capacity for accountability and leadership that assures effective and rapid response to organizational challenges.

5. Plans and processes that are non-duplicative and seamlessly connected create consistent, coordinated, and easily grasped operations.

   Process-thinking is the basic skill required in order to understand and easily review an organization's functions. CPAs learn from comparing their many client organizations that good processes lead to more efficient and effective operations. Effectively documented and linked processes also enable external consultants to spotlight problem areas and help to improve even the best organizations.

   The great leader, St. Francis of Assisi, the founder of the Franciscans (Order of Friars Minor), accomplished amazingly rapid growth and credibility for his new society. Francis established the Order in 1209. He began with seeking formal approval directly from the Pope, an unusual step for a small group of twelve. From that auspicious starting point through dispatching missionaries to virtually every corner of the globe before his death in 1226 at age 44, Francis built a strong organization based on a new kind of knighthood and a new code of honor.

Against St. Francis' protests, his disciples prevailed in establishing good infrastructure, which enabled both their expansion and their Mission based on service, simplicity and *joy*. Franciscans followed Marco Polo to the East and worked in North Africa with the Muslims. They accompanied Christopher Columbus to the New World, built their famous missions in Latin America and California, and also went to Australia with La Perouse. The infrastructure and "observances" established under St. Francis and his initial group have sustained his Mission over the centuries despite internal dissension and external challenges from Popes, Kings, and unfriendly hordes.[6,7]

Good infrastructure provides the underpinning to create an environment of trust and respect. It enables the linked communication that spreads a motivating goal throughout the organization and sustains it.

6. Compassionate behavior (i.e., seeking first to understand and then to provide for others' needs) is the most effective driver of team-focused and success-building behavior. Truly compassionate behavior also benefits every individual and every organization. A culture that reinforces this message will build and sustain the resilience DNA.

It is impossible to act with compassion for others without first respecting and honoring yourself. That's why philosophers and mental health professionals emphasize, "First, heal yourself." Good leaders constantly watch for opportunities, in each situation, to help build self-esteem within the organization — one person, one group at a time.

Build an Organization of Entrepreneurs Along the Way[8]

As you create a resilient organization, assure that there are processes to keep it entrepreneurial. The age of technology that provides information on-demand has fueled constant new challenges for organizations. The faster the access to that new information, the faster the change occurs in all markets, in all industries, and in all environments throughout our globally linked world. In order to thrive in this environment, organizations must be able to automatically and effectively respond to new information and to constantly changing customer desires. Fast reactions, fast changes, fast responses to new customer desires are the traits associated with entrepreneurs.

Being entrepreneurial also means being willing to take risks and having the strength to challenge standard practices and ignore industry politics when necessary to achieve goals. That's the kind of behavior that epitomized Phil Knight and Bill Bowerman's leadership of Nike in its rapid growth years.[9] Entrepreneurs are obsessively committed to achieving a goal to the point of risking all, even their homes, their cars, and their children's future educations.

Today these entrepreneurial traits are required for success and sustainability in all types of entities (manufacturers, governments, hospitals, retailers, schools, banks). The key to building and sustaining an entrepreneurial organization is ready access to new data from both internal and external sources coupled with a supportive environment that enables open, untethered minds. Entrepreneurial entities have a substantial advantage in achieving success because they can respond rapidly and effectively to change — they are flexible.

Today's rapid rate of change makes it even more imperative for organizations to be entrepreneurial, continually learning. Six behaviors typical of young organizations contribute to developing flexibility, the ability to obtain and absorb new data quickly, and to respond even faster.

1. **Develop an open mind.** All managers, and the people they see as potential leaders, should be actively involved in activities and issues outside their jobs, not only within but also outside their industries. The activities ideally should be in numerous directions, especially in areas where people will work for the good of others. The activities should also provide opportunities for interaction with people who have different perspectives, backgrounds, and industries and should regularly enable them to experience the *joy* of working with others to accomplish worthy goals.

2. **Update company plans continually.** Develop a process for formally reassessing the status of the organization's strategic plan as often as every six months but at least annually. The process requires updating information about new customers, competitors, and trends and automatically comparing the new information with internal issues and needs. The only efficient way to do this comparison is with a

system that keeps the underlying data readily available to all for regular reference, assessment, and use as new issues, opportunities, and needs arise.

The strategic plan should be sufficiently linked to operating processes and systems to keep it top of mind for all leaders while they focus on daily operations.

3. Focus on information and communication.
Organizations today have access to huge amounts of data. What most lack is a way to analyze and summarize the data into timely, meaningful, and concise information tailored to the needs of each department or level about their industry, organization, and other departments. More usable information will enable faster and more competent decision-making, foster continual dialogue, and also provide for more efficient information-sharing across the organization.

Awareness of relationships and of the data interaction across departments is critical to developing more effective information flows. In today's data overload environment, outside consultants, especially CPAs, are valuable in developing and analyzing data, determining what data is most useful, translating it into people-friendly summary information, and, ultimately, developing internal processes to replicate their functions.

4. Focus on achieving customer intimacy.
Entrepreneurs know their customers' needs intimately. Entrepreneurs realize that their own companies will rise or fall based on the satisfaction and success of their customers.

They ensure that everyone in their company feels the same way and knows the customers intimately.

Larger organizations can achieve the same results, but the key is to go far beyond basic market research and customer surveys. Use communication structures and processes to make customer needs real and understandable to everyone within the organization, not just to those in sales and customer service.

5. **Maximize the company's strengths and "re-infect" staff.** At the same time that companies are under pressure to be ten times smarter than they were the previous year in such areas as product design and market knowledge, they are also required to be more productive than they were the year before. They can make great strides in doing all three if they focus internal efforts on a narrower range of functions and activities in order to develop greater expertise and productivity in selected areas.

   In an attempt to show growth and to increase profits, many organizations take on functions that were previously subcontracted or they merge similar operations of acquired companies into existing departments. The result of both is that managers and supervisors become less effective as their functions broaden beyond core Mission areas.

   A return to greater use of subcontractors and consultants with specialized knowledge and skills will provide higher-level knowledge in target areas faster, help to maintain flexibility and focus within their workforce, and allow greater budgeting flexibility.

Selective outsourcing will also bring new, high-level ideas from different perspectives to the organization. Management consultants and CPAs are especially useful in identifying and evaluating areas for outsourcing or use of outside specialists.

When outside specialists are selected and managed wisely, they also can "re-infect" the company with entrepreneurial attitudes and direction. Use outside specialists, not just to accomplish a task, but also to help develop internal people while they are working on the project. Used effectively, the value-add of good outside consultants is their ability to build the strength and the competencies of internal staff with every outsourced project.

Flexibility and *ready access to new information* are the hallmarks of entrepreneurial organizations. With the above numbered concepts, even mature, bureaucratic organizations can develop these traits.

On the Way to Acting with a Collective Heartbeat, *As One*

There is no magic concept or simple principle for consistently accomplishing change. The greatest assurance lies in enhancing the ability to act with a collective heartbeat, as *ONE*. The more that ability is built within the environment and culture, the more consistent the organization's ability to achieve desired changes efficiently and successfully.

Acting As One requires an environment that builds both Ability and Desire while working on every change or goal. That easily occurs with the significant application of the three major steps — Assessment, Design, and Execution (ADE) — as described in this book, not just new Design tools.

Then the changes become part of the organization's basic fabric, growing resilience with each action taken, further infecting all its "cells" and building the ability of systems and processes to reinforce *Acting as One.*

The three substeps included in each major step of ADE (See *Chapter 7 — Infrastructure*) assure stakeholder involvement and effective communication so that the Ability to perform them efficiently penetrates the entire organization and also creates strong Desire.

A *self-less* leader is also required, one who will effectively use communication tools and processes to permeate all corners of the organization and one who also has the skills to make tough, frequently uncomfortable decisions. *Smith Desk Expeditions* is an example of what happens when great organization improvement strides are made, but there is no selfless leader.

Smith Desk Expeditions
Smith Desk Expeditions is a third-generation, family-owned furniture manufacturing business with a very successful and nationally renowned proprietary software product. The software product expedites order processing and shipping not only for the furniture industry but also for other related manufacturing companies.

Because of the specialty software, the maturity of the company, and the strong financial skills of family members, Smith Desk is highly profitable. They have invested in state-of-the-art equipment and, therefore, they serve as a job shop for many smaller manufacturing companies. A subsidiary company recycles used furniture; it has grown into a major regional recycling center for both businesses and the general public.

Each division of Smith was run as a separate company by one of the four Smith daughters and sons. Each division had independent financial and information systems. Although some of the divisions were highly profitable, some were not. A corporate-level CFO consolidated individual company financial statements into one corporate statement monthly, but details of each division's profitability, perform-ance against budget and corporate objectives, and plans for growth were obscured by the consolidation and were not shared with the siblings. As a result, there was no profit-center accountability, no central corporate strategy, no shared purchasing or infra-structure. Management functions, processes, and systems were also not shared.

The brilliant patriarch, who founded Smith and held it together while his children ran the individual companies, was in poor health and about to retire. One son, fearful of what would happen, brought in a consultant to help unify the organization through a strategic planning process. The strategic planning process was successful in linking the processes and systems, achieving transparency of all operations and results, and in improving collaboration through improved communications tools and sharing. All the companies became more effective and profitable. Smith Desk grew in reputation, market share, and profitability.

But the biggest problem was not solved by simply fixing the infrastructure issues. The biggest problem, in the words of the family's patriarch, was "my children's relationships with one another weren't fixed!" The siblings did not resolve their desires to control their individual companies; they could not agree upon a unified structure. Upon the patriarch's death, the individual companies were split among the siblings.

The problem at *Smith Desk* was that numerous leaders were unwilling to give up some control, to confront one another on management strengths and weaknesses, to make choices that might anger some, or to face tough issues publicly. It takes guts, stamina and humility to accomplish resilience, with good leaders sometimes taking personal blows in the process. In family-based organizations, where dealing with children and siblings is a daily occurrence, leadership is more difficult because of the added complexity of dealing with emotional family issues in the workplace. It frequently requires a specialty consultant/arbitrator to help resolve these tough issues.

When I learned about the *Smith Desk* situation, I realized that good tools, a great strategic plan, and effective processes will significantly improve organizations but aren't enough to ensure sustainable changes or to achieve resilience for the long term. Achieving resilience also requires an environment of trust, which is enabled by a self-less leader. But, even without one, the organization's environment can be improved significantly by practicing effective Assessment, Design, and Execution on every new project. Negative behaviors will be replaced with positive forces and tools. The potential for success of individual efforts will substantially increase even though the organization's ultimate goal of resilience is not achieved.

Wisdom and Strength – To Reach Unity/Resilience

So, where does DNA come in? The Resilience DNA is built by embedding Desire and Ability with every project undertaken, so that the resilience-building behaviors can continue despite leadership changes and organizational crises. A self-less leader can establish and link Desire and Ability and begin to embed a culture of selflessness, of always looking towards the greater good, in order to accomplish unity.

Unity feeds on itself; it is self-perpetuating. With unity in its culture, the organization builds and maintains resilience. Then, when bad leaders come or major crises occur, the organization, like the healthy human body fighting cancer, will be strong enough to survive the attack. Like the body, the right combination of strong ingredients, physical and emotional, enables the organization to heal and sustain its strength.

It takes a great leader, with wisdom, physical and emotional strength, and selflessness — desire for a greater good — to start the process towards unity. Great leaders, with both left- and right-brain ability[10] and with high emotional intelligence that helps to assure humility[11], are not born. They are forged with the fire of tough life experiences and with belief in a higher power who provides strength when life events challenge them. They use their personal strength to help build the organizational Desire and Ability that leads to group wisdom and strength.

Wisdom matters for nothing without strength; strength is misused without wisdom. A great leader isn't afraid to share authority and responsibility, to bring in outsiders as catalysts when necessary. A great leader is comfortable seeking help from and giving credit to others, especially a Higher Power.

A great leader with wisdom and strength reflects joy and spreads it throughout the organization. Joy is infectious; it is the wonder glue, the link, the secret sauce. It enables the constant building of Desire and Ability that leads to both wisdom and strength and results in unity — organizational resilience. St. Francis' friars spread throughout the world and have lasted for 800 years because their joy, despite constant internal conflicts, was infectious. The joy of Clive Charles affected his women's soccer team for a decade beyond his death; its alumnae now infect the new women's soccer team, the Portland Thorns, and the entire city of Portland. Attendance at their games far surpasses that of any other team in the new women's soccer league. Despite almost insurmountable setbacks during the finals, the Thorns won the inaugural National Women's Soccer League championship on August 1, 2013.

You can't sustain health — in mind, in body, or in any organizational body — without joy. When joy goes, health also deteriorates. Selflessness, as part of human nature through invocation of a higher power, naturally breeds joy.

Joy comes from a Higher Power — we can fight joy, deny it or ignore it. Or we can accept it, recognize it for its power, and share it. It just comes, unbidden. Once joy is received, it is hard to destroy because joy, which follows wisdom and strength, is performance-enhancing. It is the fuel of resilience. Organizational resilience is built while constructing the dual base of Desire and Ability, as described in these chapters, but it takes a self-less leader to enable the fertile environment for joy to take hold and reverberate throughout the organization.

Resilience/Unity Leads to Joy

By now, you should understand that **Resilience = Unity (Acting as One, with a Collective Heartbeat)**. And that true unity leads to joy. The greater the unity, the greater the resilience.

Unity, a collective heartbeat, is achieved with organizational wisdom and strength. The greater the collective **Wisdom and Strength**, the more likely the entity is to achieve a collective heartbeat, as the indomitable ant kingdoms[12], winning teams like the University of Portland Pilots, the Oregon Ducks, and Phil Knight and Bill Bowerman's Nike all demonstrate.

Accomplish Wisdom and Strength by building **Desire and Ability**. Through approaching every project with the intention of building this dual base, you can easily establish desire and ability one step at a time. Organizations can do this automatically, if they have the skills with tools and the experience in establishing trust internally. With most organizations, building desire and ability with every project is not difficult, but it requires focused, conscious attention and resources.

Resilience is the result of unity, *acting with a collective heartbeat*. Without unity, we are all more or less like twelve scared men in an upper room, waiting for disaster and almost certain death at the hands of the authorities. It wasn't until these ordinary men from humble backgrounds were suddenly inspired and "fired up" with unity from a Higher Power and with Trust in one another: They received the courage to speak to crowds of skeptical, angry people in languages they didn't previously know and the desire to leave families and jobs to travel to far-off places in order to accomplish their Mission.[13]

It is unity — with one another and with the Higher Power — that enables individuals to take risks, to innovate, to work zealously to accomplish the Mission and achieve the Vision. Unity enables resilience and, ultimately, the Joy of working for a greater good that sustains resilience.

People Empowerment — to create Desire

$+$

Effective Infrastructure — to build Ability

$+$

Selfless Leader — to enable group Wisdom
and Strength

$=$ Resilience

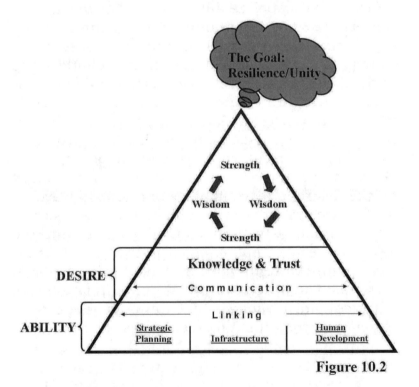

Figure 10.2

Notes

Preface

1. Peter M. Senge, *The Fifth Discipline – The Art & Practice of The Learning Organization,* (New York: Doubleday/ Currency), 1990.
2. James Belasco, *Teaching the Elephant to Dance,* (New York: Crown Publishers, Inc,), 1990.
3. John Quay, *Diagnostic Interviewing for Consultants and Auditors,* (Quay Associates), 1986.

Introduction: Wonder Glue

1. Ken Goe, "A Perfect Response by the Ducks," *The Oregonian,* October 31, 2010.
2. Kenny Moore, *Bowerman and the Men of Oregon – The Story of Oregon's Legendary Coach and Nike's Cofounder,* (Rodale Inc), 2006.
3. E.O. Wilson, *Anthill,* (W.W. Norton & Company, Inc.), 2010.
4. Biomimicry Institute, "What is Biomimicry, "On www. biomimicryinstitute.org, Accessed on January 2, 2012.
5. Alissa Walker, "Biomimicry Challenge: IDEO Taps Octopi and Flamingos to Reorganize the USGBC," On www.fastcompany.com/node/1643489, on May 10, 2010, accessed on February 16, 2011.
6. Ken Goe, "Oregon 48, Arizona 29: Civil War all that stands between Ducks and BCS title game," *The Oregonian,* November 26, 2010.
7. Brian Doyle, "The Joy", *Portland – The University of Portland Magazine,* Spring 2006.

Chapter 1: Common Knowledge

1. Tom Davenport, "Enterprise 2.0: The New, New Knowledge Management," *Harvard Business Online,* February 19, 2008.
2. Andrew McAfee, "Enterprise 2.0: The Dawn of Emergent Collaboration," *Sloan Management Review,* Spring 2006.
3. Eric Garland, "Peak Intel: How So-Called Strategic Intelligence Actually Makes Us Dumber," *Atlantic Monthly,* April 5, 2012.

4. Sun Tzu, *The Art of War*, (World Publications Group, Inc.), 2007.
5. Daniel Goleman, "Emotional Intelligence," *Harvard Business Review*, January 2004.
6. Daniel Goleman, *Emotional Intelligence – Why It Can Matter More Than IQ*, (Bantam Books), 1995 & 2005.

Chapter 2: Chemistry 101

1. Peter M. Senge, *The Fifth Discipline – The Art & Practice of The Learning Organization,* (New York: Doubleday/Currency), 1990.
2. Kenny Moore, *Bowerman and the Men of Oregon – The Story of Oregon's Legendary Coach and Nike's Cofounder,* (Rodale Inc), 2006.
3. Ken Goe, "Oregon Football: Now, it's come to this; the "natty' is on the line in next week's Civil War," *The Oregonian*, November 27, 2010.
4. Abby Haight, *AS ONE, a championship season,* (Gibbons & Haight), 2006.
5. Daniel Goleman, "Emotional Intelligence," *Harvard Business Review*, January 2004.
6. Daniel Goleman, *Emotional Intelligence – Why It Can Matter More Than IQ*, (Bantam Books), 1995 & 2005.
7. Jim Collins, *Good to Great*, (New York: HarperCollins Publishers, Inc.), 2001.
8. Daniel H. Pink, *A Whole New Mind*, (New York: Riverhead Books), 2005.
9. The Suran Group, *Innovation Transfer in the Professional Services Industry,* 1997.

Chapter 3: The New Art of War

1. Sandra Suran (Speaker),"Fear is the Villain, Courage is the Antidote"(Presentation), Battle Ground, WA, (February 25, 2003).
2. Peter M. Senge, *The Fifth Discipline Fieldbook,* (New York: Doubleday), 1994.
3. Peter M. Senge, *The Fifth Discipline – The Art & Practice of The Learning Organization,* (New York: Doubleday/Currency), 1990.
4. Katherine Martin, *Women of Courage – Inspiring Stories from the Women Who Lived Them,* (California: New World Library), 1999.

5. Valley Catholic Elementary School, See "Providing Opportunities for Each Child To Learn and Grow," On http://www.valleycatholic.org/page. cfm?p=748
6. Peter M. Senge, *The Fifth Discipline – The Art & Practice of The Learning Organization,* (New York: Doubleday/Currency), 1990.
7. Jackie Babicky, On http://www.bettersmarter richer.com
8. Chris Argyris and Donald Schön, *Theory in Practice – Increasing Professional Effectiveness,* (San Francisco, Ca: Jossey & Boss), 1974.

Chapter 4: Real Involvement

1. Jason Jennings, *Less is More,* (New York: Penguin Group), 2002.
2. Rafael Aguayo, *Dr. Deming – The American Who Taught the Japanese About Quality,* (New York: Fireside), 1991.
3. Webster's New World Dictionary, Third College Edition, (North America, Simon & Schuster), 1988.
4. Sandra Suran, "How to Implement Change Effectively," *The Journal of Corporate Accounting & Finance,"* (Wiley & Sons), 2003.

Chapter 5: Process Power

1. Jeff Mapes, "Mail Vote faces little peril from fraud case," *The Oregonian,* November 11, 2012.
2. Sandra Suran, Small Business Report to the State of Oregon, 1989.
3. Baldrige.com, *The Benefits of Process Thinking,* Retrieved May 19, 2010, from www.Baldrige.com.

Chapter 6: Strategic Vision

1. CBS News [Television Broadcast], "Ted Turner Looks Back," February 11, 2009.
2. [Interview], "Garrett Smith 2007 National Coach of the Year," *Portland - The University of Portland Magazine,* Spring 2008.
3. Aaron Fentress, "Chip Kelly Leaves Oregon," *The Oregonian,* January 16, 2013.
4. Peter M. Senge, *The Fifth Discipline – The Art & Practice of The Learning Organization,* (New York: Doubleday/Currency), 1990.

5. Gary Hamel and C.K. Prahalad, *Competing for the Future – Breakthrough strategies for seizing control of your industry and creating the markets of tomorrow*, (Harvard Business School Press), 1994.

Chapter 7: Infrastructure

1. Sandra Suran, "How To Implement Change Effectively," *Journal of Corporate Accounting & Finance*, (Wiley & Sons), 2003.

Chapter 8: People Focus

1. Sandra Suran, (Speaker), "How to Accomplish Change in a Bureaucratic Culture," Dean's Institute, Jackson Hole, WY, August 4, 2002.
2. Sandra Suran, "How To Implement Change Effectively," *Journal of Corporate Accounting & Finance*, (Wiley & Sons), 2003.
3. John Quay, *Diagnostic Interviewing for Consultants and Auditors*, (Quay Associates), 1986.

Chapter 9: Selflessness

1. Jim Collins, *Good to Great*, (New York: HarperCollins Publishers, Inc.), 2001.
2. Daniel Goleman, "Emotional Intelligence," *Harvard Business Review*, January 2004.
3. Daniel Goleman, *Emotional Intelligence – Why It Can Matter More Than IQ*, (Bantam Books), 1995 & 2005.
4. Larry Johnson and Bob Phillips, *Absolute Honesty – Building a Corporate Culture That Values Straight Talk and Rewards Integrity*, (American Management Association), 2003.
5. Katherine Martin, *Those Who Dare – Real People, Real Courage...and what we learn from them*, (California: New World Library), 2004.
6. Brian Doyle, "The Joy," *Portland – The University of Portland Magazine*, Spring, 2006.
7. Sandra Suran, "The Decline of Strategic Decision Making," The Suran Group Blog, www.surangroup.com, April 7, 2012.
8. Paul Zimmerman, "Smartest Man in Football," *Sports Illustrated*, August 29, 1988.

9. Chris Mortensen, "Smartest Man in Football," retrieved from http://espn.go.com/premium/nfl/columns/mortensen_chris/502653.html, April 26, 2000.
10. Aaron Fentress, "Meteoric rise, lasting imprint," *The Oregonian*, January 17, 2013.

Chapter 10: The Resilient Organization

1. Brian Doyle, "The Joy," *Portland – The University of Portland Magazine*, Spring, 2006.
2. Sandra Suran, (Speaker), "Ethics after Enron/Anderson – Restoring the Faith," Portland, Oregon, October 2, 2002.
3. Sandra Suran, (Speaker), "The Enron Implosion – Auditors: Victims or Accomplices," Enron Symposium, Oregon State University, Corvallis, Oregon, April 15, 2002.
4. John Quay, *Diagnostic Interviewing for Consultants and Auditors*, (Quay Associates), 1986.
5. Stanford Encyclopedia of Philosophy, "Wisdom," http://plato.stanford.edu/entries/wisdom/, January 8, 2007, Retrieved on April 6, 2013.
6. Jon M. Sweeney, *The Road to Assisi – The Essential Biography of St. Francis*, (Paraclete Press), 2004.
7. Julien Green, *God's Fool – The Life and Times of Francis of Assisi*, (Harper & Row), 1983.
8. Sandra Suran, "Thinking Like an Entrepreneur – To Accomplish Constant Change," *CPA Management Consultant, AICPA Newsletter of Management Consulting*, Summer, 1995.
9. Kenny Moore, *Bowerman and the Men of Oregon – The Story of Oregon's Legendary Coach and Nike's Cofounder*, (Rodale Inc.), 2006.
10. Daniel Pink, *A Whole New Mind – Why Right-Brainers Will Rule The Future*, (Riverhead Books), 2006.
11. Daniel Goleman, *Emotional Intelligence – Why It Can Matter More Than IQ*, (Bantam Books), 1995 & 2005.
12. E.O. Wilson, *Anthill*, (W.W. Norton & Company, Inc.), 2010.
13. The New American Bible, Saint Joseph Edition, *Acts of the Apostles*, (Catholic Book Publishing Co), 1992.

Index of Stories

About the Author

Sandra A. Suran, principal of The Suran Group, former founding partner of Suran & Company, and also former partner with KPMG Peat Marwick, is a broadly experienced and highly accomplished Change Management/Implementation Consultant. Sandra's background as a CPA auditor, over twenty-five years as a process improvement and organizational development consultant, and extensive Board leadership experience provided her with diverse, deep expertise. This enabled her to help accomplish major change in hundreds of private companies, not-for-profit organizations, and governmental agencies.

Sandra has assisted organizations in a wide variety of industries, including healthcare, education, finance, construction, manufacturing and distribution, arts, and professional services. Her integration of the people dynamics, infrastructure, and other resources and systems helped to achieve successful changes that lasted far beyond her involvement.

Sandra's awards and high-level appointments attest to her special skills and experience. Here are a few highlights:

- Selected by U.S. Small Business Administration as National Advocate of the Year

- Selected as President of the National Association of State Boards of Accountancy (NASBA)

- Appointed as Director of the Portland Branch, Federal Reserve Bank of San Francisco; Vice Chairman of the San Francisco Bank's Advisory Council on Small Business and Agriculture; Co-Chair of the Federal Reserve Bank's National Conferences on Small Business and Agriculture

239

- Appointed by the Governor as Oregon Small Business Advocate to develop and implement small business initiatives for Oregon and to lead development and approval of legislation

- Honored with the Abigail Scott Duniway Award for Outstanding Contributions to the Status of Women in Oregon

Sandra is a frequent writer and speaker on effectively accomplishing change, strategic and operations planning, alliances, Board governance, future trends, managing change, and entrepreneurial economics.

Sandra lives in Portland, Oregon. In addition to her passion for helping organizations and the people in them, she also enjoys the symphony, hiking, and cooking for friends. Her greatest joys are her children and four grandchildren.

Appendix

Pathway to Improvement
Summary of Process

Page	Phase 1 - Assess Situation	Phase 2 - Design Solutions	Phase 3 - Execute
Chap 7: 146	1. Collect information about current status		
152	2. Summarize and analyze issues		
154	3. Discuss and debate – inform and involve		
155		4. Collect information for alternatives	
158		5. Summarize and analyze information	
Chap 8: 174		6. Develop alternatives; select solutions and strategies	
179			7. Research and design implementation process and structure
184			8. Summarize implementation; develop tools
186			9. Implement, monitor, improve

241

Future Books

The Resilient Organization:
Entrepreneurs in a
Bureaucratic Environment

Building for the Future:
Resilient Organizations for Social Good

Proactive Governance:
Boosting Resilience from a Macro View

More Information

(website) www.thesurangroup.com
(book website) www.resiliencedna.com
(blog) www.surangroup.com

www.facebook.com/pages/The-Suran-
Group/308827226902
www.linkedin.com/in/sandrasuran
www.twitter.com/thesurangroup